IØ16Ø769

Editor's Note

Benjamin Jowett's early translation of Plato's *Apology* is remarkably free of Victorianisms, and brings to life the figure of Socrates with an easy colloquialism. Almost the entire dialogue is actually a monologue, battling the demons, real or imaginary, that had haunted him for decades.

The record we have is Plato's rendition of Socrates' words and the court proceedings. Our best assumption is that Plato himself was there—he places himself as a mute audience member in the dialogue. Are Plato's words direct from Socrates' mouth? Common Greek practice by Herodotus, Thucydides and others, was to recreate scenes or even entire speeches from the past as they might have happened; today we would describe taking those liberties with history as docudrama. The later dialogues that Plato wrote featuring Socrates have led critics to wonder how much in these texts represent Plato, a systematic philosophizer, and how much could be attributed to actual statements made by Socrates, the perennial seeker.

Xenophon also wrote a work about the same trial; he was not present. The text of his account, with his interpretation of events, follows the Supplement section; however, the Supplement material in this volume does not deal directly with the Xenophon text.

This text continues Jowett's usage of the "universal he"; variant editions are in the planning stage at Bandanna Books. I welcome comments on whether gender-variant texts for this and other classics written before the 20th century would be useful in classroom settings, or in ebook formats.

Sasha Newborn
bandanna@cox.net
August 2011

CONTENTS

Supplement Edition

The Apology of Socrates
&
The Crito

in the 1864 translation of
Benjamin Jowett

edited by
Sasha Newborn

and the text of

Xenophon's
Apology of Socrates

BANDANNA BOOKS · SANTA BARBARA

Supplement Edition: Apology of Socrates & Crito
copyright © 2011 Bandanna Books
ISBN 978-0-942208-39-9

This volume is intended for class use with *The Apology of Socrates &
The Crito* (ISBN 978-0-942208-05-4)

BANDANNA BOOKS COLLEGE TITLES

SAPPHO: THE POEMS.* Greece's greatest lyric poet. $9.95

AREOPAGITICA: FREEDOM OF THE PRESS.* John Milton. Censorship
ancient and modern. $9.95

THE APOLOGY OF SOCRATES, & THE CRITO.* Plato. $9.95

THE FIRST DETECTIVE: THREE STORIES. EDGAR ALLAN POE. Poe's ama-
teur detective Dupin was the model for Sherlock Holmes.
$12.95

DON'T PANIC: THE PROCRASTINATOR'S GUIDE TO WRITING AN EFFECTIVE
TERM PAPER. Steven Posusta. $11.95

MITOS Y LEYENDAS DE MÉXICO/MYTHS AND LEGENDS OF MEXICO. Luis
Leal. Twenty origin stories and history. Color plates by Álvaro
Ángel Suman. $39.50

GHAZALS OF GHALIB. Ghalib's witty couplets, arguing with God, his
beloved. $9.95

THE MERCHANT OF VENICE. William Shakespeare. Modernized by
Rachel Burke. $11.95

GANDHI ON THE GITA. M.K. Gandhi explains the Bhagavad Gita chapter by chapter. $9.95

LEAVES OF GRASS, 1855 edition.* Walt Whitman. $11.95

ITALIAN FOR OPERA LOVERS. Italian opera terms. $5.95

DANTE & HIS CIRCLE. D. G. Rossetti. Italian love sonnets & Dante's
Vita Nuova. $12.95

Order through our website at www.bandannabooks.com/bbooks
College Bookstores: fax orders for 5+ copies to 805-899-2145

*Teacher supplements available.

THE APOLOGY OF SOCRATES

How have you felt, O Athenians, at hearing the speeches of my accusers, I cannot tell; but I know that their persuasive words almost made me forget who I was, such was the effect of them; and yet they have hardly spoken a word of truth. But many as their falsehoods were, there was one of them which quite amazed me: I mean when they told you to be upon your guard, and not to let yourselves be deceived by the force of my eloquence. They ought to have been ashamed of saying this, because they were sure to be detected as soon as I opened my lips and displayed my deficiency; they certainly did appear to be most shameless in saying this, unless by the force of eloquence they mean the force of truth; for then I do indeed admit that I am eloquent. But in how different a way from theirs! Well, as I was saying, they have hardly uttered a word, or not more than a word, of truth; but you shall hear from me the whole truth: not, however, delivered after their manner, in a set oration duly ornamented with words and phrases. No, indeed! but I shall use the words and arguments which occur to me at the moment; for I am certain that this is right, and that at my time of life I ought not to be appearing before you, O people of Athens, in the character of a juvenile orator: let no one expect this of me. And I must beg of you to grant me one favor, which is this—If you hear me using the same words in my defense which I have been in the habit of using, and which most of you may have heard in the agora, and at the tables of the money-changers, or anywhere else, I would ask you not to be surprised at this, and not to interrupt me. For I am more than seventy years of age, and this is the first time that I have ever appeared in a court of law, and I am quite a stranger to the ways of the place; and therefore I would have you regard me as if I were really a stranger, whom you would excuse if he spoke in his native tongue, and after the fashion of his country: that I think is not an unfair request. Never mind the manner, which may or may not be good; but think only of the justice of my cause, and give heed to that: let the judge decide justly and the speaker speak truly.

And first, I have to reply to the older charges and to my first accusers, and then I will go on to the later ones. For I have had many accusers, who accused me of old, and their false charges have continued during many years; and I am more afraid of them than of Anytus and his associates, who are dangerous, too, in their own way. But far more dangerous are these, who began when you were children, and took possession of your minds with their falsehoods, telling of one Socrates, a wise man, who speculated about the heaven above, and searched into the earth beneath, and made the worse appear the better cause.

These are the accusers whom I dread; for they are the circulators of this rumor, and their hearers are too apt to fancy that speculators of this sort do not believe in the gods. And they are many, and their charges against me are of ancient date, and they made them in days when you were impressible—in childhood, or perhaps in youth—and the cause when heard went by default, for there was none to answer. And hardest of all, their names I do not know and cannot tell; unless in the chance case of a comic poet. But the main body of these slanderers who from envy and malice have wrought upon you—and there are some of them who are convinced themselves, and impart their convictions to others—all these, I say, are most difficult to deal with; for I cannot have them up here, and examine them, and therefore I must simply fight with shadows in my own defense, and examine when there is no one who answers. I will ask you then to assume with me, as I was saying, that my opponents are of two kinds—one recent, the other ancient; and I hope that you will see the propriety of my answering the latter first, for these accusations you heard long before the others, and much oftener.

Well, then, I will make my defense, and I will endeavor in the short time which is allowed to do away with this evil opinion of me which you have held for such a long time and I hope that I may succeed, if this be well for you and me and that my words may find favor with you. But I know that to accomplish this is not easy—I quite see the nature of the task. Let the event be as God wills: in obedience to the law I make my defense.

I will begin at the beginning and ask what the accusation is which has given rise to this slander of me, and which has encouraged Meletus to proceed against me. What do the slanderers say? They shall be my prosecutors, and I will sum up their words in an affidavit: Socrates is an evil-doer, and a curious person, who searches into things under the earth and in heaven, and he makes the worse appear the better cause; and he teaches the aforesaid doctrines to others. That is the nature of the accusation, and that is what you have seen yourselves in the comedy of Aristophanes, who has introduced a man whom he calls Socrates, going about and saying that he can walk in the air, and talking a deal of nonsense concerning matters of which I do not pretend to know either much or little—not that I mean to say anything disparaging of anyone who is a student of natural philosophy. I should be very sorry if Meletus could lay that to my charge. But the simple truth is, O Athenians, that I have nothing to do with these studies. Very many of those here present are witnesses to the truth of this, and to them I appeal. Speak then, you who have heard me, and tell your neighbors whether any of you have ever known me hold forth in few words or in many upon matters of this sort.... You hear their answer. And from what they say of this you will be able to judge of the truth of the rest.

As little foundation is there for the report that I am a teacher, and take money; that is no more true than the other. Although, if a man is able to teach, I honor him for being paid. There is Gorgias of Leontium, and Prodicus of Ceos, and Hippias of Elis, who go the round of the cities, and are able to persuade the young men to leave their own citizens, by whom they might be taught for nothing, and come to them, whom they not only pay, but are thankful if they may be allowed to pay them.

There is actually a Parian philosopher residing in Athens, of whom I have heard; and I came to hear of him in this way: I met a man who has spent a world of money on the Sophists, Callias the son of Hipponicus, and, knowing that he had sons, I asked him:

SOCRATES: Callias, if your two sons were foals or calves, there would be no difficulty in finding someone to put over them; we should hire a trainer of horses, or a farmer probably, who would improve and perfect them in their own proper virtue and excellence; but as they are human beings, whom are you thinking of placing over them? Is there anyone who understands human and political virtue? You must have thought about this, as you have sons; is there anyone?"

CALLIAS: There is.

S: Who is he? And of what country? And what does he charge?

C: Evenus the Parian, he is the man, and his charge is five minae.

S: Happy is Evenus, I said to myself, if he really has this wisdom, and teaches at such a modest charge. Had I the same, I should have been very proud and conceited; but the truth is that I have no knowledge of the kind, O Athenians.

I dare say that someone will ask the question, Why is this, Socrates, and what is the origin of these accusations of you: for there must have been something strange which you have been doing? All this great fame and talk about you would never have arisen if you had been like other people: tell us, then, why this is, as we should be sorry to judge hastily of you.

Now, I regard this as a fair challenge, and I will endeavor to explain to you the origin of this name of "wise," and of this evil fame. Please to attend, then. And although some of you may think that I am joking, I declare that I will tell you the entire truth.

People of Athens, this reputation of mine has come of a certain sort of wisdom which I possess. If you ask me what kind of wisdom, I reply, such wisdom as is by man, for to that extent I am inclined to believe that I am wise; whereas the men of whom I was speaking have a superhuman wisdom, which I may fail to describe, because I have it not myself; and he who says that I have, speaks falsely, and is taking away my character.

And here, O people of Athens, I must beg you not to interrupt me, even if I seem to say something extravagant. For the word which I will speak is not mine. I will refer you to a witness who is worthy of credit, and will tell you about my wisdom—whether I have any, and of what sort—and that witness shall be the god of Delphi.

You must have known Chaerephon; he was early a friend of mine, and also a friend of yours, for he shared in the recent exile of the people, and returned with you. Well, Chaerephon, as you know, was very impetuous in all his doings, and he went to Delphi and boldly asked the oracle to tell him whether—as I was saying, I must beg you not to interrupt—he asked the oracle to tell him whether there was anyone wiser than I was, and the Pythian prophetess answered that there was none wiser. Chaerephon is dead himself; but his brother, who is in court, will confirm the truth of this story.

Why do I mention this? Because I am going to explain to you why I have such an evil name. When I heard the answer, I said to myself, What can the god mean? and what is the interpretation of this riddle? for I know that I have no wisdom, small or great. What can she mean when she says that I am the wisest of men? And yet he is a god, and cannot lie; that would be against his nature.

After a long consideration, I at last thought of a method of trying the question. I refl ected that if I could only find a person wiser than myself, then I might go to the god with a refutation in my hand. I should say to him, Here is a man who is wiser than I am; but you said that I was the wisest.

Accordingly I went to one who had the reputation of wisdom, and observed him—his name I need not mention; he was a politician whom I selected for examination—and the result was as follows: When I began to talk with him, I could not help thinking that he was not really wise, although he was thought wise by many, and wiser still by himself; and I went and tried to explain to him that he thought himself wise, but was not really wise; and the consequence was that he hated me, and his enmity was shared by several who were present and heard me.

So I left him, saying to myself, as I went away: Well, although I do not suppose that either of us knows anything really beautiful and good, I am better off than he is—for he knows nothing, and thinks that he knows; I neither know nor think that I know. In this latter particular, then, I seem to have slightly the advantage of him.

Then I went to another who had still higher philosophical pretensions, and my conclusion was exactly the same. I made another enemy of him, and of many others besides him.

After this I went to one man after another, being not unconscious of the enmity which I provoked, and I lamented and feared this: but necessity was laid upon me—the word of God, I thought, ought to be considered first. And I said to myself, Go I must to all who appear to know, and find out the meaning of the oracle. And I swear to you, Athenians, by the dog I swear!—for I must tell you the truth—the result of my mission was just this: I found that the men most in repute were all but the most foolish; and that some inferior men were really wiser and better.

I will tell you the tale of my wanderings and of the "Herculean" labors, as I may call them, which I endured only to find at last the oracle irrefutable. When I left the politicians, I went to the poets; tragic, dithyrambic, and all sorts. And there, I said to myself, you will be detected; now you will find out that you are more ignorant than they are.

Accordingly I took them some of the most elaborate passages in their own writings, and asked what was the meaning of them—thinking that they would teach me something. Will you believe me? I am almost ashamed to speak of this, but still I must say that there is hardly a man present who would not have talked better about their poetry than they did themselves. That showed me in an instant that not by wisdom do poets write poetry, but by a sort of genius and inspiration; they are like diviners or soothsayers who also say many fine things, but do not understand the meaning of them. And the poets appeared to me to be much in the same case; and I further observed that upon the strength of their poetry they believed themselves to be the wisest of people in other things in which they were not wise. So I departed, conceiving myself to be superior to them for the same reason that I was superior to the politicians.

At last I went to the artisans, for I was conscious that I knew nothing at all, as I may say, and I was sure that they knew many fine things; and here I was not mistaken, for they did know many things of which I was ignorant, and in this they certainly were wiser than I was. But I observed that even the good artisans fell into the same error as the poets—because they were good workmen they thought that they also knew all sorts of high matters, and this defect in them overshadowed their wisdom—therefore I asked myself on behalf of the oracle, whether I would like to be as I was, neither having their knowledge nor their ignorance, or like them in both; and I made answer to myself and the oracle that I was better off as I was.

This investigation has led to my having many enemies of the worst and most dangerous kind, and has given occasion also to many calumnies.

And I am called wise, for my hearers always imagine that I myself possess the wisdom which I find wanting in others: but the truth is, O people of Athens, that God only is wise; and in this oracle he intends to say that human wisdom is worth little or nothing; he is not speaking of Socrates, he is only using my name as an illustration, as if he said, He, O people, is the wisest, who, like Socrates, knows that his wisdom is in truth worth nothing.

And so I go my way, obedient to the god, and search and make inquisition into the wisdom of anyone, whether citizen or stranger, who appears to be wise; and if he is not wise, then in vindication of the oracle I show him that he is not wise; and this occupation quite absorbs me, and I have no time to give either to any public matter of interest or to any concern of my own, but I am in utter poverty by reason of my devotion to the god.

There is another thing—young men of the richer classes, who have not much to do, come about me of their own accord; they like to hear the pretenders examined, and they often imitate me, and examine others themselves; there are plenty of persons, as they soon enough discover, who think that they know something, but really know little or nothing; and then those who are examined by them instead of being angry with themselves are angry with me: This confounded Socrates, they say, this villainous misleader of youth!— and then if somebody asks them, Why, what evil does he practice or teach? they do not know, and cannot tell; but in order that they may not appear to be at a loss, they repeat the ready-made charges which are used against all philosophers about teaching things up in the clouds and under the earth, and having no gods, and making the worse appear the better cause; for they do not like to confess that their pretense of knowledge has been detected—which is the truth; and as they are numerous and ambitious and energetic, and are all in battle array and have persuasive tongues, they have filled your ears with their loud and inveterate calumnies.

And this is the reason why my three accusers, Meletus and Anytus and Lycon, have set upon me; Meletus, who has a quarrel with me on behalf of the poets; Anytus, on behalf of the craftspeople; Lycon, on behalf of the rhetoricians. And, as I said at the beginning, I cannot expect to get rid of this mass of calumny all in a moment.

And this, O people of Athens, is the truth and the whole truth; I have concealed nothing, I have dissembled nothing. And yet, I know that this plainness of speech makes them hate me, and what is their hatred but a proof that I am speaking the truth?—this is the occasion and reason of their slander against me, as you will find out either in this or in any future enquiry.

I have said enough in my defense against the first class of my accusers; I turn to the second class who are headed by Meletus, that good and patriotic man, as he calls himself. And now I will try to defend myself against them: these new accusers must also have their affidavit read. What do they say? Something of this sort: That Socrates is a doer of evil, and corrupter of the youth; and he does not believe in the gods of the state, and has other new divinities of his own. That is the sort of charge; and now let us examine the particular counts. He says that I am a doer of evil, who corrupt the youth; but I say, people of Athens, that Meletus is a doer of evil, and the evil is that he makes a joke of a serious matter, and is too ready at bringing other people to trial from a pretended zeal and interest about matters in which he really never had the smallest interest. And the truth of this I will endeavor to prove to you.

Come here, Meletus, and let me ask a question of you. You think a great deal about the improvement of youth?

MELETUS: Yes, I do.

SOCRATES: Tell the judges, then, who is their improver; for you must know, as you have taken the pains to discover their corrupter, and are citing and accusing me before them. Speak, then, and tell the judges who their improver is. Observe, Meletus, that you are silent, and have nothing to say. But is not this rather disgraceful, and a very considerable proof of what I was saying, that you have no interest in the matter?

Speak up, friend, and tell us who their improver is.

M: The laws.

S: But that, my good sir, is not my meaning. I want to know who the man is, who, in the first place, knows the laws.

M: The judges, Socrates, who are present in court.

S: What, do you mean to say, Meletus, that they are able to instruct and improve youth?

M: Certainly they are.

S: What, all of them, or some only and not others?

M: All of them.

S: By the goddess Hera, that is good news! There are plenty of improvers, then. And what do you say of the audience—do they improve them?

M; Yes, they do.

S: And the senators?

M: Yes, the senators improve them.

S: But perhaps the ecclesiasts corrupt them?—or do they too improve them?

M: They improve them.

S: Then every Athenian improves and elevates them; all with the exception of myself; and I alone am their corrupter? Is that what you affirm?

M: That is what I stoutly affirm.

S: I am very unfortunate if that is true. But suppose I ask you a question: Would you say that this also holds true in the case of horses? Does one person do them harm and all the world good? Is not the exact opposite of this true? One person is able to do them good, or at least not many; the trainer of horses, that is to say, does them good, and others who have to do with them rather injure them? Is not that true, Meletus, of horses, or of any other animals? Yes, certainly. Whether you or Anytus say yes or no, that is no matter. Happy indeed would be the condition of youth if they had one corrupter only, and all the rest of the world were their improvers. And you, Meletus, have sufficiently shown that you never had a thought about the young; your carelessness is seen in your not caring about the matters spoken of in this very indictment.

And now, Meletus, I must ask you another question: Which is better, to live among bad citizens, or among good ones? Answer, friend, I say; for that is a question is one which may be easily answered. Do not the good do their neighbors good, and the bad do them evil?

M: Certainly.

S: And is there anyone who would rather be injured than benefited by those who live with him? Answer, my good friend, the law requires you to answer—does anyone like to be injured?

M: Certainly not.

S: And when you accuse me of corrupting and deteriorating the youth, do you allege that I corrupt them intentionally or unintentionally?

M: Intentionally, I say.

S: But you have just admitted that the good do their neighbors good, and the evil do them evil. Now, is that a truth which your superior wisdom has recognized thus early in life, and am I, at my age, in such darkness and ignorance as not to know that if a man with whom I have to live is corrupted by me, I am very likely to be harmed by him, and yet I corrupt him, and intentionally, too; that is what you are saying, and of that you will never persuade me or any other human being. But either I do not corrupt them, or I corrupt them unintentionally, so that on either view of the case you lie. If my offense is unintentional, the law has no cognizance of unintentional offenses: you ought to have taken me privately, and warned and admonished me; for if I had been better advised, I should have left off doing what I only did unintentionally—no doubt I should; whereas you hated to converse with me or teach me, but you indicted me in this court, which is a place not of instruction, but of punishment.

I have shown, Athenians, as I was saying, that Meletus has no care at all, great or small, about the matter. But still I should like to know, Meletus, in what I am affirmed to corrupt the young. I suppose you mean, as I infer from your indictment, that I teach them not to acknowledge the gods which the state acknowledges, but some other new divinities or spiritual agencies in their stead. These are the lessons which corrupt the youth, as you say.

M: Yes, that I say emphatically.

S: Then, by the gods, Meletus, of whom we are speaking, tell me and the court, in somewhat plainer terms, what you mean! for I do not as yet understand whether you affirm that I teach others to acknowledge some gods, and therefore do believe in gods and am not an entire atheist—this you do not lay to my charge—but only that they are not the same gods which the city recognizes—the charge is that they are different gods. Or, do you mean that I am an atheist simply, and a teacher of atheism?

M: I mean the latter—that you are a complete atheist.

S: That is an extraordinary statement, Meletus. Why do you say that?

Do you mean that I do not believe in the godhead of the sun or moon, which is the common creed of all people?

M: I assure you, judges, that he does not believe in them; for he says that the sun is stone, and the moon earth.

S: Friend Meletus, you think that you are accusing Anaxagoras: and you have but a bad opinion of the judges, if you fancy them ignorant to such a degree as not to know that these doctrines are found in the books of Anaxagoras the Clazomenian, who is full of them. And these are the doctrines which the youth are said to learn of Socrates, when there are not unfrequently exhibitions of them at the theater (price of admission one drachma at the most); and they might cheaply purchase them, and laugh at Socrates if he pretends to father such eccentricities. And so, Meletus, you really think that I do not believe in any god?

M: I swear by Zeus that you believe absolutely in none at all.

S: You are a liar, Meletus, not believed even by yourself. I cannot help thinking, people of Athens, that Meletus is reckless and impudent, and that he has written this indictment in a spirit of mere wantonness and youthful bravado. Has he not compounded a riddle, thinking to try me?

He said to himself: I shall see whether this wise Socrates will discover my ingenious contradiction, or whether I shall be able to deceive him and the rest of them. For he certainly does appear to me to contradict himself in the indictment as much as if he said that Socrates is guilty of not believing in the gods, and yet of believing in them—but this is surely a piece of fun.

I should like you, O people of Athens, to join me in examining what I conceive to be his inconsistency; and do you, Meletus, answer. And I must remind you that you are not to interrupt if I speak in my accustomed manner:

Did ever a person, Meletus, believe in the existence of human things, and not of human beings? ...I wish, people of Athens, that he would answer, and not be always trying to get up an interruption. Did ever anyone believe in horsemanship, and not in horses? or in fl ute-playing, and not in fl ute-players? No, my friend; I will answer to you and to the court, as you refuse to answer for yourself. There is no one who ever did. But now please to answer the next question: Can a person believe in spiritual and divine agencies, and not in spirits or demigods?

M: He cannot.

S: I am glad that I have extracted that answer, by the assistance of the court; nevertheless you swear in the indictment that I teach and believe in divine or spiritual agencies (new or old, no matter for that); at any rate, I believe in spiritual agencies, as you say and swear in the affidavit; but if I believe in divine beings, I must believe in spirits or demigods; is not that true? Yes, that is true, for I may assume that your silence gives assent to that. Now what are spirits or demigods? are they not either gods or the children of gods? Is that true?

M: Yes, that is true.

S: But this is just the ingenious riddle of which I was speaking: the demigods or spirits are gods, and you say first that I don't believe in gods, and then again that I do believe in gods; that is, if I believe in demigods.

For if the demigods are the illegitimate children of gods, whether by the nymphs or by any other mothers, as is thought, that, as all will allow, necessarily implies the existence of their parents. You might as well affirm the existence of mules, and deny that of horses and asses.

Such nonsense, Meletus, could only have been intended by you as a trial of me. You have put this into the indictment because you had nothing real of which to accuse me. But no one who has a particle of understanding will ever be convinced by you that the same people can believe in divine and superhuman things, and yet not believe that there are gods and demigods and heroes.

I have said enough in answer to the charge of Meletus: any elaborate defense is unnecessary; but as I was saying before, I certainly have many enemies, and this is what will be my destruction if I am destroyed; of that I am certain; not Meletus, nor yet Anytus, but the envy and detraction of the world, which has been the death of many good people, and will probably be the death of many more; there is no danger of my being the last of them.

Someone will say: And are you not ashamed, Socrates, of a course of life which is likely to bring you to an untimely end? To him I may fairly answer: There you are mistaken: a man who is good for anything ought not to calculate the chance of living or dying; he ought only to consider whether in doing anything he is doing right or wrong—acting the part of a good man or of a bad.

Whereas, upon your view, the heroes who fell at Troy were not good for much, and the son of Thetis above all, who altogether despised danger in comparison with disgrace; and when his goddess mother said to him, in his eagerness to slay Hector, that if he avenged his companion Patroclus, and slew Hector, he would die himself—"Fate," as she said, "waits upon you next after Hector"; he, hearing this, utterly despised danger and death, and instead of fearing them, feared rather to live in dishonor, and not to avenge his friend. "Let me die next," he replies, "and be avenged of my enemy, rather than abide here by the beaked ships, a scorn and a burden of the earth."

Had Achilles any thought of death and danger? For wherever a man's place is, whether the place which he has chosen or that in which he has been placed by a commander, there he ought to remain in the hour of danger; he should not think of death, or of anything, but of disgrace.

And this, O people of Athens, is a true saying.

Strange, indeed, would be my conduct, O people of Athens, if I, who, when I was ordered by the generals whom you chose to command me at Potidaea and Amphipolis and Delium, remained where they placed me, like any other soldier, facing death—if, I say, now, when, as I conceive and imagine, God orders me to fulfill the philosopher's mission of searching into myself and other people, I were to desert my post through fear of death, or any other fear; that would indeed be strange, and I might justly be arraigned in court for denying the existence of the gods, if I disobeyed the oracle because I was afraid of death: then I should be fancying that I was wise when I was not wise. For this fear of death is indeed the pretense of wisdom, and not real wisdom, being the appearance of knowing the unknown; since no one knows whether death, which they in their fear apprehend to be the greatest evil, may not be the greatest good. Is there not here conceit of knowledge, which is a disgraceful sort of ignorance? And this is the point in which, as I think, I am superior to people in general, and in which I might perhaps fancy myself wiser than other people—that whereas I know but little of the world below, I do not suppose that I know: but I do know that injustice and disobedience to a better, whether God or man, is evil and dishonorable, and I will never fear or avoid a possible good rather than a certain evil.

And therefore, if you let me go now and reject the counsels of Anytus, who said that if I were not put to death I ought not to have been prosecuted, and that if I escape now, your sons will all be utterly ruined by listening to my words—if you say to me, Socrates, this time we will not mind Anytus, and will let you off, but upon one condition, that you are not to inquire and speculate in this way any more, and that if you are caught doing this again you shall die—if this was the condition on which you let me go, I should reply: People of Athens, I honor and love you; but I shall obey God rather than you, and while I have life and strength I shall never cease from the practice and teaching of philosophy, exhorting anyone whom I meet after my manner, and convincing him, saying: O my friend, why do you, who are a citizen of the great and mighty and wise city of Athens, care so much about laying up the greatest amount of money and honor and reputation, and so little about wisdom and truth and the greatest improvement of the soul, which you never regard or heed at all? Are you not ashamed of this?

And if the person with whom I am arguing, says: Yes, but I do care; I do not depart or let him go at once; I interrogate and examine and cross-examine him, and if I think that he has no virtue, but only says that he has, I reproach him with undervaluing the greater, and overvaluing the less. And this I should say to everyone whom I meet, young and old, citizen and alien, but especially to the citizens, inasmuch as they are my brothers and sisters.

For this is the command to God, as I would have you know; and I believe that to this day no greater good has ever happened in the state than my service to the God. For I do nothing but go about persuading you all, old and young alike, not to take thought for your persons or your properties, but first and chiefl y to care about the greatest improvement of the soul. I tell you that virtue is not given by money, but that from virtue come money and every other good of humanity, public as well as private.

This is my teaching, and if this is the doctrine which corrupts the youth, my infl uence is ruinous indeed. But if anyone says that this is not my teaching, he is speaking an untruth. Wherefore, O people of Athens, I say to you, do as Anytus bids or not as Anytus bids, and either acquit me or not; but whatever you do, know that I shall never alter my ways, not even if I have to die many times.

People of Athens, do not interrupt, but hear me; there was an agreement between us that you should hear me out. And I have something more to say, at which you may be inclined to cry out; but I beg that you will not do this. I would have you know, that if you kill such a one as I am, you will injure yourselves more than you will injure me. Meletus and Anytus will not injure me: they cannot; for it is not in the nature of things that a bad man should injure a better than himself. I do not deny that he may, perhaps, kill him, or drive him into exile, or deprive him of civil rights; and he may imagine, and others may imagine, that he is doing him a great injury: but in that I do not agree with him; for the evil of doing as Anytus is doing—of unjustly taking away another's life—is greater far.

And now, Athenians, I am not going to argue for my own sake, as you may think, but for yours, that you may not sin against the God, or lightly reject his boon by condemning me. For if you kill me you will not easily find another like me, who, if I may use such a ludicrous figure of speech, am a sort of gadfl y, given to the state by the God; and the state is like a great and noble horse who is tardy in him motions owing to him very size, and requires to be stirred into life. I am that gadfl y which God has given the state, and all day long and in all places am always fastening upon you, arousing and persuading and reproaching you.

And as you will not easily find another like me, I would advise you to spare me. I dare say that you may feel irritated at being suddenly awakened when you are caught napping; and you may think that if you were to strike me dead as Anytus advises, which you easily might, then you would sleep on for the remainder of your lives, unless God in him care of you gives you another gadfl y.

And that I am given to you by God is proved by this: that if I had been like other people, I should not have neglected all my own concerns, or patiently seen the neglect of them during all these years, and have been doing yours, coming to you individually, like a father or elder brother, exhorting you to regard virtue; this, I say, would not be like human nature. And had I gained anything, or if my exhortations had been paid, there would have been some sense in that: but now, as you will perceive, not even the impudence of my accusers dares to say that I have ever exacted or sought pay of anyone; they have no witness of that. And I have a witness of the truth of what I say; my poverty is a sufficient witness.

Someone may wonder why I go about in private, giving advice

and busying myself with the concerns of others, but do not venture to come forward in public and advise the state. I will tell you the reason of this.

You have often heard me speak of an oracle or sign which comes to me, and is the divinity which Meletus ridicules in the indictment. This sign I have had ever since I was a child. The sign is a voice which comes to me and always forbids me to do something which I am going to do, but never commands me to do anything, and this is what stands in the way of my being a politician. And rightly, as I think. For I am certain, O people of Athens, that if I had engaged in politics, I should have perished long ago, and done no good either to you or to myself.

And don't be offended at my telling you the truth: for the truth is, that no man who goes to war with you or any other multitude, honestly struggling against the commission of unrighteousness and wrong in the state, will save him life; he who will really fight for the right, if he would live even for a little while, must have a private station and not a public one.

I can give you as proofs of this, not words only, but deeds, which you value more than words. Let me tell you a passage of my own life, which will prove to you that I should never have yielded to injustice from any fear of death, and that if I had not yielded I should have died at once. I will tell you a story—tasteless, perhaps, and commonplace, but nevertheless true. The only office of state which I ever held, O people of Athens, was that of senator; the tribe Antiochis, which is my tribe, had the presidency at the trial of the generals who had not taken up the bodies of the slain after the battle of Arginusae; and you proposed to try them all together, which was illegal, as you all thought afterwards; but at the time I was the only one of the prytanes who was opposed to the illegality, and I gave my vote against you; and when the orators threatened to impeach and arrest me, and have me taken away, and you called and shouted, I made up my mind that I would run the risk, having law and justice with me, rather than take part in your injustice because I feared imprisonment and death. This happened in the days of the democracy.

But when the oligarchy of the Thirty was in power, they sent for me and four others into the rotunda, and bade us bring Leon the Salaminian from Salamis, as they wanted to execute him. This was a specimen of the sort of commands which they were always giving with the view of implicating as many as possible in their crimes;

and then I showed, not in word only but in deed, that, if I may be allowed to use such an expression, I cared not a straw for death, and that my only fear was the fear of doing an unrighteous or unholy thing. For the strong arm of that oppressive power did not frighten me into doing wrong; and when we came out of the rotunda the other four went to Salamis and fetched Leon, but I went quietly home. For which I might have lost my life, had not the power of the Thirty shortly afterwards come to an end. And to this many will witness.

Now, do you really imagine that I could have survived all these years, if I had led a public life, supposing that like a good man I had always supported the right and had made justice, as I ought, the first thing? No indeed, people of Athens, neither I nor any other.

But I have been always the same in all my actions, public as well as private, and never have I yielded any base compliance to those who are slanderously termed my disciples, or to any other. For the truth is that I have no regular disciples: but if anyone likes to come and hear me while I am pursuing my mission, whether he be young or old, he may freely come. Nor do I converse with those who pay only, and not with those who do not pay; but anyone, whether he be rich or poor, may ask and answer me and listen to my words; and whether he turns out to be a bad person or a good one, that cannot be justly laid to my charge, as I never taught anything. And if anyone says that he has ever learned or heard anything from me in private which all the world has not heard, I should like you to know that he is speaking an untruth.

But I shall be asked, Why do people delight in continually conversing with you? I have told you already, Athenians, the whole truth about this: they like to hear the cross-examination of the pretenders to wisdom; there is amusement in it. And this is a duty which the God has imposed upon me, as I am assured by oracles, visions, and in every sort of way in which the will of divine power was ever signified to anyone.

This is true, O Athenians; or, if not true, would be soon refuted. For if I am really corrupting the youth, and have corrupted some of them already, those of them who have grown up and have become sensible that I gave them bad advice in the days of their youth should come forward as accusers, and take their revenge; and if they do not like to come themselves, some of their relatives, fathers, brothers, or other kinfolk, should say what evil their families have suffered at my hands.

Now is their time.

Many of them I see in the court. There is Crito, who is of the same age and of the same deme with myself, and there is Critobulus his son, whom I also see. Then again there is Lysanias of Sphettus, who is the father of Aeschines—he is present; and also there is Antiphon of Cephisus, who is the father of Epigenes; and there are the brothers of several who have associated with me. There is Nicostratus the son of Theosdotides, and the brother of Theodotus (now Theodotus himself is dead, and therefore he, at any rate, will not seek to stop him); and there is Paralus the son of Demodocus, who had a brother Theages; and Adeimantus the son of Ariston, whose brother Plato is present; and Aeantodorus, who is the brother of Apollodorus, whom I also see. I might mention a great many others, some of whom Meletus should have produced as witnesses in the course of his speech; and let him still produce them, if he has forgotten; I will make way for him. And let him say, if he has any testimony of the sort which he can produce. Nay, Athenians, the very opposite is the truth. For all these are ready to witness on behalf of the corrupter, of the destroyer of their kindred, as Meletus and Anytus call me; not the corrupted youth only—there might have been a motive for that—but their uncorrupted elder relatives. Why should they too support me with their testimony? Why, indeed, except for the sake of truth and justice, and because they know that I am speaking the truth, and that Meletus is lying.

Well, Athenians, this and the like of this is all the defense which I have to offer. Yet a word more. Perhaps there may be someone who is offended at me, when he calls to mind how he himself on a similar, or even a less serious occasion, had recourse to prayers and supplications with many tears, and how he produced his children in court, which was a moving spectacle, together with a posse of his relations and friends; whereas I, who am probably in danger of my life, will do none of these things. Perhaps this may come into his mind, and he may be set against me, and vote in anger because he is displeased at this.

Now, if there be such a person among you, which I am far from affirming, I may fairly reply to him: My friend, I am a man, and like other men, a creature of fl esh and blood, and not of wood or stone, as Homer says; and I have a family, yes, and sons, O Athenians, three in number, one of whom is growing up, and the two others are still young; and yet I will not bring any of them here in order to petition you for an acquittal. And why not? Not from any self-will or disregard of you. Whether I am or am not afraid of death is another question, of which I will not now speak. But my reason simply is, that I feel such conduct to be discreditable to myself, and you, and the whole state.

A man who has reached my years, and who has a name for wisdom, whether deserved or not, ought not to demean himself. At any rate, the world has decided that Socrates is in some way superior to other people. And if those among you who are said to be superior in wisdom and courage, and any other virtue, demean themselves in this way, how shameful is their conduct! I have seen men of reputation, when they have been condemned, behaving in the strangest manner: they seemed to fancy that they were going to suffer something dreadful if they died, and that they could be immortal if you only allowed them to live; and I think they were a dishonor to the state, and that any stranger coming in would say of them that the most eminent people of Athens, to whom the Athenians themselves give honor and command, are no better than housewives.

And I say that these things ought not to be done by those of us who are of reputation; and if they are done, you ought not to permit them; you ought rather to show that you are more inclined to condemn, not the person who is quiet, but the person who gets up a doleful scene and makes the city ridiculous.

But, setting aside the question of dishonor, there seems to be something wrong in petitioning a judge, and thus procuring an acquittal, instead of informing and convincing him. For his duty is, not to make a present of justice, but to give judgment; and he has sworn that he will judge according to the laws, and not according to his own good pleasure; and neither he nor we should get into the habit of perjuring ourselves—there can be no piety in that.

Do not then require me to do what I consider dishonorable and impious and wrong, especially now, when I am being tried for impiety on the indictment of Meletus. For if, people of Athens, by force of persuasion and entreaty, I could overpower your oaths, then I should be teaching you to believe that there are no gods, and convict myself, in my own defense, of not believing in them. But that is not the case; for I do believe that there are gods, and in a far higher sense than that in which any of my accusers believe in them. And to you and to God I commit my cause, to be determined by you as is best for you and me.

There are many reasons why I am not grieved, O people of Athens, at the vote of condemnation. I expected this, and am only surprised that the votes are so nearly equal; for I had thought that the majority against me would have been far larger; but now, had thirty votes gone over to the other side, I should have been acquitted. And I may say that I have escaped Meletus. And I may say more; for without the assistance of Anytus and Lycon, he would not have had a fifth part of the votes, as the law requires, in which case he would have incurred a fine of a thousand drachmae, as is evident.

And so he proposes death as the penalty. And what shall I propose on my part, O people of Athens? Clearly that which is my due. And what is that which I ought to pay or to receive? What shall be done to the man who has never had the wit to be idle during his whole life; but has been careless of what the many care about— wealth, and family interests, and military offices, and speaking in the assembly, and magistracies, and plots, and parties. Refl ecting that I was really too honest a man to follow in this way and live, I did not go where I could do no good to you or to myself; but where I could do the greatest good privately to every one of you, there I went, and sought to persuade everyone among you, that he must look to himself, and seek virtue and wisdom before he looks to his private interests, and look to the state before he looks to the interests of the state; and that this should be the order which he observes in all his actions. What shall be done to such a man?

Doubtless some good thing, O people of Athens, if he has his reward; and the good should be of a kind suitable to him. What would be a reward suitable to a poor fellow who is your benefactor, who desires leisure that he may instruct you? There can be no more fitting reward than maintenance in the prytaneum, O people of Athens, a reward which he deserves far more than the citizen who has won the prize at Olympia in the horse or chariot race, whether the chariots were drawn by two horses or by many. For I am in want, and he has enough; and he only gives you the appearance of happiness, and I give you the reality.

And if I am to estimate the penalty justly, I say that maintenance in the prytaneum is the just return.

Perhaps you think that I am braving you in saying this, as in what I said before about the tears and prayers. But that is not the case. I speak rather because I am convinced that I never intentionally wronged anyone, although I cannot convince you of that—for we have had a short conversation only; but if there were a law at Athens, such as there is in other cities, that a capital cause should not be decided in one day, then I believe that I should have convinced you; but now the time is too short. I cannot in a moment refute great slanders; and, as I am convinced that I never wronged another, I will assuredly not wrong myself. I will not say of myself that I deserve any evil, or propose any penalty. Why should I? Because I am afraid of the penalty of death which Meletus proposes? When I do not know whether death is a good or an evil, why should I propose a penalty which would certainly be an evil? Shall I say imprisonment? And why should I live in prison, and be the slave of the magistrates of the year—of the Eleven?

Or shall the penalty be a fine, and imprisonment until the fine is paid? There is the same objection. I should have to lie in prison, for money I have none, and cannot pay. And if I say exile (and this may possibly be the penalty which you will affix), I must indeed be blinded by the love of life, if I were to consider that when you, who are my own citizens, cannot endure my discourses and words, and have found them so grievous and odious that you would have done with them, others are likely to endure me. No indeed, people of Athens, that is not very likely.

And what a life should I lead, at my age, wandering from city to city, living in ever-changing exile, and always being driven out! For I am quite sure that into whatever place I go, as here so also there, the young people will come to me; and if I drive them away, their elders will drive me out at their desire; and if I let them come, their fathers and friends will drive me out for their sakes.

Someone will say: Yes, Socrates, but cannot you hold your tongue, and then you may go into a foreign city, and no one will interfere with you?

Now I have great difficulty in making you understand my answer to this.

For if I tell you that this would be a disobedience to a divine command, and therefore that I cannot hold my tongue, you will not believe that I am serious; and if I say again that the greatest human good is daily to converse about virtue, and all that concerning which you hear me examining myself and others, and that the life which is unexamined is not worth living—that you are still less likely to believe.

And yet I say what is true, although a thing of which it is hard for me to persuade you. Moreover, I am not accustomed to think that I deserve any punishment. Had I money I might have proposed to give you what I had, and had been none the worse. But you see that I have none, and can only ask you to proportion the fine to my means. However, I think that I could afford a mina, and therefore I propose that penalty: Plato, Crito, Critobulus, and Apollodorus, my friends here, bid me say thirty minae, and they will be the sureties. Well, then, say thirty minae, let that be the penalty; for that they will be ample security to you.

•

Not much time will be gained, O Athenians, in return for the evil name which you will get from the detractors of the city, who will say that you killed Socrates, a wise man; for they will call me wise, even though I am not wise, when they want to reproach you.

If you had waited a little while, your desire would have been fulfilled in the course of nature. For I am far advanced in years, as you may perceive, and not far from death. I am speaking now only to those of you who have condemned me to death.

And I have another thing to say to them: You think that I was convicted through deficiency of words—I mean, that if I had thought fit to leave nothing undone, nothing unsaid, I might have gained an acquittal.

Not so; the deficiency which led to my conviction was not of words—certainly not. But I had not the boldness or impudence or inclination to address you as you would have liked me to address you, weeping and wailing and lamenting, and saying and doing many things which you have been accustomed to hear from others, and which, as I say, are unworthy of me.

But I thought that I ought not to do anything common or mean in the hour of danger: nor do I now repent of the manner of my defense, and I would rather die having spoken after my manner, than speak in your manner and live. For neither in war nor yet at law ought anyone to use every way of escaping death. For often in battle there is no doubt that if a soldier will throw away his arms, and fall on his knees before his pursuers, he may escape death; and in other dangers there are other ways of escaping death, if a man is willing to say and do anything.

The difficulty, my friends, is not in avoiding death, but in avoiding unrighteousness; for that runs faster than death. I am old and move slowly, and the slower runner has overtaken me, and my accusers are keen and quick, and the faster runner, who is unrighteousness, has overtaken them.

And now I depart hence condemned by you to suffer the penalty of death, and they too go their ways condemned by the truth to suffer the penalty of villainy and wrong; and I must abide by my award—let them abide by theirs. I suppose that these things may be regarded as fated—and I think that they are well.

And now, O people who have condemned me, I would prophesy to you; for I am about to die, and that is the hour in which persons are gifted with prophetic power. And I prophesy to you who are my murderers, that immediately after my death punishment far heavier than you have infl icted on me will surely await you. Me you have killed because you wanted to escape the accuser, and not to give an account of your lives. But that will not be as you suppose: far otherwise. For I say that there will be more accusers of you than there are now; accusers whom hitherto I have restrained: and as they are younger they will be more severe with you, and you will be more offended at them. For if you think that by killing men you can avoid the accuser censuring your lives, you are mistaken; that is not a way of escape which is either possible or honorable; the easiest and the noblest way is not to be crushing others, but to be improving yourselves. This is the prophecy which I utter before my departure to the judges who have condemned me.

Friends, who would have acquitted me, I would like also to talk with you about this thing which has happened, while the magistrates are busy, and before I go to the place at which I must die. Stay then a while, for we may as well talk with one another while there is time. You are my friends, and I should like to show you the meaning of this event which has happened to me. O my judges—for you I may truly call judges—I should like to tell you of a wonderful circumstance. Hitherto the familiar oracle within me has constantly been in the habit of opposing me even about trifl es, if I was going to make a slip or error about anything; and now as you see there has come upon me that which may be thought, and is generally believed to be, the last and worst evil. But the oracle made no sign of opposition, either as I was leaving my house and going out in the morning, or when I was going up into this court, or while I was speaking, at anything which I was going to say; and yet I have often been stopped in the middle of a speech, but now in nothing I either said or did touching this matter has the oracle opposed me. What do I take to be the explanation of this? I will tell you. I regard this as a proof that what has happened to me is a good, and that those of us who think that death is an evil are in error. This is a great proof to me of what I am saying, for the customary sign would surely have opposed me had I been going to evil and not to good.

Let us reflect in another way, and we shall see that there is great reason to hope that death is a good; for one of two things: either death is a state of nothingness and utter unconsciousness, or, as people say, there is a change and migration of the soul from this world to another.

Now, if you suppose that there is no consciousness, but a sleep like the sleep of him who is undisturbed even by the sight of dreams, death will be an unspeakable gain. For if a person were to select the night in which his sleep was undisturbed even by dreams, and were to compare with this the other days and nights of his life, and then were to tell us how many days and nights he] had passed in the course of his life better and more pleasantly than this one, I think that anyone, I will not say a private person, but even the great king will not find many such days or nights, when compared with the others. Now if death is like this, I say that to die is gain; for eternity is then only a single night. But if death is the journey to another place, and there, as people say, all the dead are, what good, O my friends and judges, can be greater than this? If indeed when the pilgrim arrives in the world below, he is delivered from the professors of justice in this world, and finds the true judges who are said to give judgment there, Minos and Rhadamanthus and Aeacus and Triptolemus, and other children of God who were righteous in their own life, that pilgrimage will be worth making.

What would not a person give if he might converse with Orpheus and Musaeus and Hesiod and Homer? No, if this be true, let me die again and again. I, too, shall have a wonderful interest in a place where I can converse with Palamedes, and Ajax the son of Telamon, and other heroes of old, who have suffered death through an unjust judgment; and there will be no small pleasure, as I think, in comparing my own sufferings with theirs. Above all, I shall be able to continue my search into true and false knowledge; as in this world, so also in the next; I shall find out who is wise, and who pretends to be wise, and is not. What would not a fellow give, O judges, to be able to examine the leader of the great Trojan expedition; or Odysseus or Sisyphus, or numberless others, men and women too! What infinite delight would there be in conversing with them and asking them questions! For in that world they do not put a person to death for this; certainly not. For besides being happier in that world than in this, they will be immortal, if what is said is true.

Wherefore, O judges, be of good cheer about death, and know this of a truth—that no evil can happen to a good person, either in life or after death. He and his are not neglected by the gods; nor has my own approaching end happened by mere chance.

But I see clearly that to die and be released was better for me; and therefore the oracle gave no sign. For which reason, also, I am not angry with my accusers or my condemners; they have done me no harm, although neither of them meant to do me any good; and for this I may gently blame them.

Still, I have a fabor to ask of them. When my sons are grown up, I would ask you, O my friends, to punish them; and I would have you trouble them, as I have troubled you, if they seem to care about riches, or anything, more than about virtue; or if they pretend to be something when they are really nothing—then reprove them, as I have reproved you, for not caring about that for which they ought to care, and thinking that they are something when they are really nothing. And if you do this, both I and my sons will have received justice at your hands.

The hour of departure has arrived, and we go our ways—I to die, and you to live. Which is better God only knows.

•

THE CRITO

CHARACTERS: Socrates, Crito
SCENE: The prison of Socrates

SOCRATES: Why have you come at this hour, Crito? It must be quite early.

CRITO: Yes, certainly.

S: What is the exact time?

C: The dawn is breaking.

S: I wonder the keeper of the prison would let you in.

C: He knows me because I often come, Socrates; moreover, I have done him a kindness.

S: And are you only just come?

C: No, I came some time ago.

S: Then why did you sit and say nothing, instead of awakening me at once?

C: Why, indeed, Socrates, I myself would rather not have all this sleeplessness and sorrow. But I have been wondering at your peaceful slumbers, and that was the reason why I did not awaken you, because I wanted you to be out of pain. I have always thought you happy in the calmness of your temperament; but never did I see the like of the easy, cheerful way in which you bear this calamity.

S: Why, Crito, when a person has reached my age he ought not to be repining at the prospect of death.

C: And yet other old people find themselves in similar misfortunes, and age does not prevent them from repining.

S: That may be. But you have not told me why you come at this early hour.

C: I come to bring you a message which is sad and painful; not, as I believe, to yourself, but to all of us who are your friends, and saddest of all to me.

S: What? I suppose that the ship has come from Delos, on the arrival of which I am to die?

C: No, the ship has not actually arrived, but she will probably be here today, as persons who have come from Sunium tell me that they left her there; and therefore tomorrow, Socrates, will be the last day of your life.

S: Very well, Crito; if such is the will of God, I am willing; but my belief is that there will be a delay of a day.

C: Why do you say this?

S: I will tell you. I am to die on the day after the arrival of the ship?

C: Yes; that is what the authorities say.

S: But I do not think that the ship will be here until tomorrow; this I gather from a vision which I had last night, or rather only just now, when you fortunately allowed me to sleep.

C: And what was the nature of the vision?

S: There came to me the likeness of a woman, fair and comely, clothed in white raiment, who called to me and said:

O Socrates, "The third day hence, to fertile Phthia shall you go.
[Homer, *Iliad*]

C: What a singular dream, Socrates!

S: There can be no doubt about the meaning, Crito, I think.

C: Yes; the meaning is only too clear. But, O! my beloved Socrates, let me entreat you once more to take my advice and escape. For if you die I shall not only lose a friend who can never be replaced, but there is another evil: people who do not know you and me will believe that I might have saved you if I had been willing to give money, but that I did not care. Now, can there be a worse disgrace than this—that I should be thought to value money more than the life of a friend? For the many will not be persuaded that I wanted you to escape, and that you refused.

S: But why, my dear Crito, should we care about the opinion of the many? Good people, and they are the only persons who are worth considering, will think of these things truly as they happened.

C: But do you see, Socrates, that the opinion of the many must be regarded, as is evident in your own case, because they can do the very greatest evil to anyone who has lost their good opinion.

S: I only wish, Crito, that they could; for then they could also do the greatest good, and that would be well. But the truth is, that they can do neither good nor evil: they cannot make a man either wise or make him foolish; and whatever they do is the result of chance.

C: Well, I will not dispute about that; but please to tell me, Socrates, whether you are not acting out of regard to me and your other friends: are you not afraid that if you escape hence we may get into trouble with the informers for having stolen you away, and lose either the whole or a great part of our property; or that even a worse evil may happen to us?

Now, if this is your fear, be at ease; for in order to save you, we ought surely to run this, or even a greater risk; be persuaded, then, and do as I say.

S: Yes, Crito, that is one fear which you mention, but by no means the only one.

C: Fear not, there are persons who at no great cost are willing to save you and bring you out of prison; and as for the informers, you may observe that they are far from being exorbitant in their demands; a little money will satisfy them. My means, which, as I am sure, are ample, are at your service, and if you have a scruple about spending all mine, here are strangers who will give you the use of theirs; and one of them, Simmias the Theban, has brought a sum of money for this very purpose; and Cebes and many others are willing to spend their money too.

I say, therefore, do not on that account hesitate about making your escape, and do not say, as you did in the court, that you will have a difficulty in knowing what to do with yourself if you escape. For people will love you in other places to which you may go, and not in Athens only; there are friends of mine in Thessaly, if you like to go to them, who will value and protect you, and no Thessalian will give you any trouble. Nor can I think that you are justified, Socrates, in betraying your own life when you might be saved; this is playing into the hands of your enemies and destroyers; and moreover I should say that you were betraying your children; for you might bring them up and educate them; instead of which you go away and leave them, and they will have to take their chance; and if they do not meet with the usual fate of orphans, there will be small thanks to you. No one should bring children into the world who is unwilling to persevere to the end in their nurture and education.

But you are choosing the easier part, as I think, not the better and manlier, which would rather have become one who professes virtue in all his actions, like yourself. And, indeed, I am ashamed not only of you, but of us who are your friends, when I refl ect that this entire business of yours will be attributed to our want of courage.

The trial need never have come on, or might have been brought to another issue; and the end of all, which is the crowning absurdity, will seem to have been permitted by us, through cowardice and baseness, who might have saved you, as you might have saved yourself, if we had been good for anything (for there was no difficulty in escaping); and we did not see how disgraceful, Socrates, and also miserable all this will be to us as well as to you. Make your mind up then, or rather have your mind already made up, for the time of deliberation is over, and there is only one thing to be done, which must be done, if at all, this very night, and which any delay will render all but impossible; I beseech you therefore, Socrates, to be persuaded by me, and to do as I say.

S: Dear Crito, your zeal is invaluable, if a right one; but if wrong, the greater the zeal the greater the evil; and therefore we ought to consider whether these things shall be done or not. For I am and always have been one of those natures who must be guided by reason, whatever the reason may be which upon refl ection appears to me to be the best; and now that this fortune has come upon me, I cannot put away the reasons which I have before given: the principles which up to now I have honored and revered I still honor, and unless we can find other and better principles on the instant, I am certain not to agree with you; no, not even if the power of the multitude could infl ict many more imprisonments, confiscations, deaths, frightening us like children with hobgoblin terrors.

But what will be the fairest way of considering the question? Shall I return to your old argument about the opinions of people? some of which are to be regarded, and others, as we were saying, are not to be regarded. Now, were we right in maintaining this before I was condemned? And has the argument which was once good now proved to be talk for the sake of talking; in fact an amusement only, and altogether vanity?

That is what I want to consider with your help, Crito: whether, under my present circumstances, the argument appears to be in any way different or not; and is to be allowed by me or disallowed. That argument, which, as I believe, is maintained by many who assume to be authorities, was to the effect, as I was saying, that the opinions of some people are to be regarded, and of other people not to be regarded. Now you, Crito, are a disinterested man who is not going to die tomorrow—at least, there is no human probability of this, and you are therefore not liable to be deceived by the circumstances in which you are placed.

Tell me, then, whether I am right in saying that some opinions, and the opinions of some people only, are to be valued, and other opinions, and the opinions of other people, are not to be valued. I ask you whether I was right in maintaining this?

C: Certainly.

S: The good are to be regarded, and not the bad?

C: Yes.

S: And the opinions of the wise are good, and the opinions of the unwise are evil?

C: Certainly.

S: And what was said about another matter? Was the disciple in gymnastics supposed to attend to the praise and blame and opinion of everyone, or of one person only— his physician or trainer, whoever that was?

C: Of one person only.

S: And he ought to fear the censure and welcome the praise of that one only, and not of the many?

C: That is clear.

S: And he ought to live and train, and eat and drink in the way which seems good to his single master who has understanding, rather than according to the opinion of all other people put together?

C: True.

S: And if he disobeys and disregards the opinion and approval of the one, and regards the opinion of the many who have no understanding, will he not suffer evil?

C: Certainly he will.

S: And what will the evil be, whither tending and what affecting, in the disobedient person?

C: Clearly, affecting the body; that is what is destroyed by the evil.

S: Very good; and is not this true, Crito, of other things which we need not separately enumerate? In the matter of just and unjust, fair and foul, good and evil, which are the subjects of our present
34

consultation, ought we to follow the opinion of the many and to fear them; or the opinion of the one man who has understanding, and whom we ought to fear and reverence more than all the rest of the world: and whom deserting we shall destroy and injure that principle in us which may be assumed to be improved by justice and deteriorated by injustice; is there such a principle?

C: Certainly there is, Socrates.

S: Take a parallel instance: if, acting under the advice of those who have no understanding, we destroy that which is improved by health and deteriorated by disease—when that has been destroyed, I say, would life be worth having? And that is—the body?

C: Yes.

S: Could we live, having an evil and corrupted body?

C: Certainly not.

S: And will life be worth having, if that higher part of a person be depraved, which is improved by justice and deteriorated by injustice?

Do we suppose that principle, whatever it may be in a person, which has to do with justice and injustice, to be inferior to the body?

C: Certainly not.

S: More honored, then?

C: Far more honored.

S: Then, my friend, we must not regard what the many say of us: but what he, the one man who has understanding of just and unjust, will say, and what the truth will say. And therefore you begin in error when you advise that we should regard the opinion of the many about just and unjust, good and evil, honorable and dishonorable. Well, someone will say, but the many can kill us.

C: Yes, Socrates; that will clearly be the answer.

S: That is true: but still I find with surprise that the old argument is, as I conceive, unshaken as ever. And I should like to know whether I may say the same of another proposition—that not life, but a good life, is to be chiefl y valued?

C: Yes, that also remains.

S: And a good life is equivalent to a just and honorable one—that holds also?

C: Yes, that holds.

S: From these premises I proceed to argue the question whether I ought or ought not to try and escape without the consent of the Athenians: and if I am clearly right in escaping, then I will make the attempt; but if not, I will abstain. The other considerations which you mention, of money and loss of character and the duty of educating children, are, as I fear, only the doctrines of the multitude, who would be as ready to call people to life, if they were able, as they are to put them to death—and with as little reason.

But now, since the argument has thus far prevailed, the only question which remains to be considered is, whether we shall do rightly either in escaping or in suffering others to aid in our escape and paying them in money and thanks, or whether we shall not do rightly; and if the latter, then death or any other calamity which may ensue on my remaining here must not be allowed to enter into the calculation.

C: I think that you are right, Socrates; how then shall we proceed?

S: Let us consider the matter together, and do you either refute me if you can, and I will be convinced; or else cease, my dear friend, from repeating to me that I ought to escape against the wishes of the Athenians: for I am extremely desirous to be persuaded by you, but not against my own better judgment. And now please to consider my first position, and do your best to answer me.

C: I will do my best.

S: Are we to say that we are never intentionally to do wrong, or that in one way we ought and in another way we ought not to do wrong, or is doing wrong always evil and dishonorable, as I was just now saying, and as has been already acknowledged by us? Are all our former admissions which were made within a few days to be thrown away?

And have we, at our age, been earnestly discoursing with one another all our life long only to discover that we are no better than children?

Or are we to rest assured, in spite of the opinion of the many, and in spite of consequences whether better or worse, of the truth of what was then said, that injustice is always an evil and dishonor to hum who acts unjustly? Shall we affirm that?

C: Yes.

S: Then we must do no wrong?

C: Certainly not.

S: Nor when injured injure in return, as the many imagine; for we must injure no one at all?

C: Clearly not.

S: Again, Crito, may we do evil?

C: Surely not, Socrates.

S: And what of doing evil in return for evil, which is the morality of the many—is that just or not?

C: Not just.

S: For doing evil to another is the same as injuring him?

C: Very true.

S: Then we ought not to retaliate or render evil for evil to anyone, whatever evil we may have suffered from him. But I would have you consider, Crito, whether you really mean what you are saying.

For this opinion has never been held, and never will be held, by any considerable number of persons; and those who are agreed and those who are not agreed upon this point have no common ground, and can only despise one another when they see how widely they differ. Tell me, then, whether you agree with and assent to my first principle, that neither injury nor retaliation nor warding off evil by evil is ever right.

And shall that be the premise of our argument? Or do you decline and dissent from this? For this has been of old and is still my opinion; but, if you are of another opinion, let me hear what you have to say.

If, however, you remain of the same mind as formerly, I will proceed to the next step.

C: You may proceed, for I have not changed my mind.

S: Then I will proceed to the next step, which may be put in the form of a question: Ought a person to do what he admits to be right, or ought he to betray the right?

C: He ought to do what he thinks right.

S: But if this is true, what is the application? In leaving the prison against the will of the Athenians, do I wrong any? or rather do I not wrong those whom I ought least to wrong? Do I not desert the principles which were acknowledged by us to be just? What do you say?

C: I cannot tell, Socrates; for I do not know.

S: Then consider the matter in this way: Imagine that I am about to play truant (you may call the proceeding by any name which you like), and the laws and the government come and interrogate me: *Tell us, Socrates,* they say, *what are you about? are you going by an act of yours to overturn us–the laws, and the whole state, as far as in you lies? Do you imagine that a state can subsist and not be overthrown, in which the decisions of law have no power, but are set aside and overthrown by individuals?* What will be our answer, Crito, to these and the like words? Anyone, and especially a clever rhetorician, will have a good deal to urge about the evil of setting aside the law which requires a sentence to be carried out. and we might reply, *Yes, but the state has injured us and given an unjust sentence.* Suppose I say that?

C: Very good, Socrates.

S: *And was that our agreement with you?* the law would say; *or were you to abide by the sentence of the state?* And if I were to express astonishment at their saying this, the law would probably add: *Answer, Socrates, instead of opening your eyes: you are in the habit of asking and answering questions. Tell us what complaint you have to make against us which justifies you in attempting to destroy us and the state? In the first place, did we not bring you into existence? Your father married your mother by our aid and begat you. Say whether you have any objection to urge against those of us who regulate marriage.*

None, I should reply.

Or against those of us who regulate the system of nurture and education of children, in which you were trained? Were not the laws, who have the charge of this, right in commanding your father to train you in music and gymnastic?

Right, I should reply.

Well, then, since you were brought into the world and nurtured and educated by us, can you deny in the first place that you are our child and slave, as your parents were before you? And if this is true, you are not on equal terms with us; nor can you think that you have a right to do to us what we are doing to you. Would you have any right to strike or revile or do any other evil to a parent or to your master, if you had one, when you have been struck or reviled by him, or received some other evil at his hands?–you would not say this? And because we think right to destroy you, do you think that you have any right to destroy us in return, and your country as far as in you lies? Will you, O professor of true virtue, say that you are justified in this? Has a philosopher like you failed to discover that our country is more to be valued and higher and holier far than mother or father or any ancestor, and more to be regarded in the eyes of the gods and of people of understanding? also to be soothed, and gently and reverently entreated when angry, even more than a parent, and if not persuaded, or if not persuaded, obeyed?

And when we are punished by her, whether with imprisonment or stripes, the punishment is to be endured in silence; and if she lead us to wounds or death in battle, there we follow as is right; neither may anyone yield or retreat or leave his rank, but whether in battle or in a court of law, or in any other place, he must do what his] city and his country order him; or he must change their view of what is just: and if he may do no violence to his father or mother, much less may he do violence to his country.

What answer shall we make to this, Crito? Do the laws speak truly, or do they not?

C: I think that they do.

S: Then the laws will say: *Consider, Socrates, if this is true, that in your present attempt you are going to do us wrong. For, after having brought you into the world, and nurtured and educated you, and given you and every other citizen a share in every good that we had to give, we further proclaim and give the right to every Athenian, that if he does not like us when he has come of age and has seen the ways of the city, and made our acquaintance, he may go where he pleases and take his goods with him. Any of you who does not like us and the city, and who wants to go to a colony or to any other city, may go where he likes, and take his goods with him.*

But he who has experience of the manner in which we order justice and administer the state, and still remains, has entered into an implied contract that he will do as we command him. And he who disobeys us is, as we maintain, thrice wrong; first, because in disobeying us he is disobeying his parents; secondly, because we are the authors of his education; thirdly, because he has made an agreement with us that he will duly obey our commands; and he neither obeys them nor convinces us that our commands are wrong; and we do not rudely impose them, but give him the alternative of obeying or convincing us—that is what we offer, and he does neither.

These are the sort of accusations to which, as we were saying, you, Socrates, will be exposed if you accomplish your intentions; you, above all other Athenians.

Suppose I ask, *why is this?* They will justly retort upon me that I above all other people have acknowledged the agreement. *There is clear proof,* they will say, *Socrates, that we and the city were not displeasing to you. Of all Athenians you have been the most constant resident in the city, which, as you never leave, you may be supposed to love. For you never went out of the city either to see the games, except once when you went to the Isthmus, or to any other place unless you were on military service; nor did you travel as other people do. Nor had you any curiosity to know other states or their laws; your affections did not go beyond us and our state; we were your special favorites, and you acquiesced in our government of you; and this is the city in which you begat your children, which is a proof of your satisfaction.*

Moreover, you might, if you had liked, have fixed the penalty at banishment in the course of the trial–the state which refuses to let you go now would have let you go then. But you pretended that you preferred death to exile, and that you were not grieved at death.

And now you have forgotten these fine sentiments, and pay no respect to us the laws, of whom you are the destroyer; and are doing what only a miserable slave would do, running away and turning your back upon the compacts and agreements which you made as a citizen.

And first of all answer this very question: Are we right in saying that you agreed to be governed according to us in deed, and not in word only? Is that true or not?

How shall we answer that, Crito? Must we not agree?

C: There is no help, Socrates.

S: Then will they not say: *You, Socrates, are breaking the covenants and agreements which you made with us at your leisure, not in any haste or under any compulsion or deception, but having had seventy years to think of them, during which time you were at liberty to leave the city, if we were not to your mind, or if our covenants appeared to you to be unfair.*

You had your choice, and might have gone either to Lacedaemon or Crete, which you often praise for their good government, or to some other Hellenic or foreign State. Whereas you, above all other Athenians, seemed to be so fond of the state, or, in other words, of us its laws (for who would like a state that has no laws?), that you never stirred out of it; the halt, the blind, the maimed were not more stationary in it than you were.

And now you run away and forsake your agreements. Not so, Socrates, if you will take our advice; do not make yourself ridiculous by escaping out of the city.

For just consider, if you transgress and err in this sort of way, what good will you do, either to yourself or to your friends? That your friends will be driven into exile and deprived of citizenship, or will lose their property, is tolerably certain; and you yourself, if you fl y to one of the neighboring cities, as, for example, Thebes or Megara, both of which are well governed cities, will come to them as an enemy, Socrates, and their government will be against you, and all patriotic citizens will cast an evil eye upon you as a subverter of the laws, and you will confirm in the minds of the judges the justice of their own condemnation of you.

For he who is a corrupter of the laws is more than likely to be a corrupter of the young and foolish portion of humanity.

Will you then fl ee from well-ordered cities and virtuous men? and is existence worth having on these terms?

Or will you go to them without shame, and talk to them, Socrates? And what will you say to them? What you say here about virtue and justice and institutions and laws being the best things among people? Would that be decent of you? Surely not.

But if you go away from well-governed States to Crito's friends in Thessaly, where there is great disorder and license, they will be charmed to hear the tale of your escape from prison, set off with ludicrous particulars of the manner in which you were wrapped in a goatskin or some other disguise, and metamorphosed as the fashion of runaways is–that is very likely; but will there be no one to remind you that in your old age you violated the most sacred laws from a miserable desire of a little more life?

Perhaps not, if you keep them in a good temper; but if they are out of temper you will hear many degrading things; you will live, but how?–as the fl atterer of all people, and the servant of all people; and doing what?– eating and drinking in Thessaly, having gone abroad in order that you may get a dinner.

And where will be your fine sentiments about justice and virtue then?

Say that you wish to live for the sake of your children, that you may bring them up and educate them–will you take them into Thessaly and deprive them of Athenian citizenship? Is that the benefit which you will confer upon them? Or are you under the impression that they will be better cared for and educated here if you are still alive, although absent from them; for that your friends will take care of them? Do you fancy that if you are an inhabitant of Thessaly they will take care of them, and if you an inhabitant of the other world they will not take care of them? No; but if they who call themselves friend are truly friends, they surely will.

Listen, then, Socrates, to us who have brought you up. Think not of life and children first, and of justice afterwards, but of justice first, that you may be justified before the princes of the world below. For neither will you nor any that belong to you be happier or holier or juster in this life, or happier in another, if you do as Crito bids.

Now you depart in innocence, a sufferer and not a doer of evil; a victim, not of the laws, but of people. But if you go forth, returning evil for evil, and injury for injury, breaking the covenants and agreements which you have made with us, and wronging those whom you ought least to wrong, that is to say, yourself, your friends, your country, and us, we shall be angry with you while you live, and our brethren, the laws in the world below, will receive you as an enemy; for they will know that you have done your best to destroy us. Listen, then, to us and not to Crito.

This is the voice which I seem to hear murmuring in my ears, like the sound of the flute in the ears of the mystic; that voice, I say, is humming in my ears, and prevents me from hearing any other. And I know that anything more which you may say will be vain. Yet speak, if you have anything to say.

C: I have nothing to say, Socrates.

S: Then let me follow the intimations of the will of God.

•

Supplement
to
The Apology of Socrates
& The Crito

edited by
Sasha Newborn

Supplement Edition: Apology of Socrates & Crito
copyright © 2011 Bandanna Books
ISBN 978-0-942208-39-9

This volume is intended for class use
with *The Apology of Socrates & The
Crito*, ISBN 978-0-942208-05-4.

BANDANNA BOOKS · SANTA BARBARA

Contents

Preface for Teachers

This supplement is designed to help classroom teachers by providing background and offering a variety of answers to student questions about *The Apology of Socrates & The Crito*. On the other hand, we do not presume to answer here the major issues raised by Platonic philosophy. All of philosophy is a footnote to Plato, said Alfred North Whitehead.

Instead of focusing on Plato, the emphasis here is on Socrates, taking into consideration Plato's accuracy in presenting the man Socrates. For a thorough-going answer to that question, compare this text with Xenophon's *Apology* (following the supplement is the text)—Xenophon also followed Socrates closely, but he was not present at the trial itself, as Plato was known to be. Keep in mind that this was a real trial in 399 BCE, reported by other partisans, and a subject of political controversy soon after its occurrence.

This supplement material is organized around questions, with a number of "answers" supplied. These answers do not all agree. Over the course of more than two thousand years, opinions about Socrates fluctuate as if governed by fashion. Of the modern texts about this trial, the one that impressed me most in bringing to life the politics of Athens is I.F. Stone's *The Trial of Socrates*. An old muckraker himself, Stone forces on the reader some uncomfortable ideas. Though Socrates was not an aristocrat, he was an unrepentant anti-democrat, says Stone. The issues Plato glosses over may be as important as the ones he emphasizes. Students should have a good time picking over the bones of this old philosopher.

When Benjamin Jowett translated all of Plato's dialogues, among the first he did was the *Apology of Socrates*. Late in life, Jowett decided to make a more rigorous translation. As editor, I respect his choice, but decline his offer. The fresh plain-language conversational style of Jowett's first translation transcended the blight of fastidiousness and stylishness that infected almost every Victorian writer; the first translation is perhaps still the most readable today.

One significant lapse by Jowett, and most writers before 1970, is to use a universal "he" or otherwise ignore half their readership. In this Bandanna Books text version, we respect the original. However, variant editions are in the planning stage. You may have an opinion on whether or not to use or offer such gender-inclusive variant editions in your classroom; I would be glad to hear it. Several possibilities, including he/she, s/he, hir, his/her, tey, hey, hu are under consideration. An early survey from teachers on this subject has been inconclusive. The mission of Bandanna Books is "to build a better book." Especially in our focus on classics, the issue of gender reference in works and translations comes up over and over again.

Not included in this publication are two associated dialogues, a short one, *Euthyphro*, preceding the trial, and the *Phaedo*, following the *Crito*. The *Euthyphro* engages Socrates and a young man going to trial to sue his father for the death of a slave, but does not deal with Socrates' own case. The *Phaedo*, much more substantial as a philosophical dialogue, contains a discussion of immortality and a dramatic scene of Socrates drinking the hemlock poison. I did choose to include Xenophon's account of the actual trial; would the *Phaedo* be helpful as well, or is that beyond the scope of your interest in the *Apology*?

Sasha Newborn
August 2011

What is important about the *Apology*?

Plato's *Apology* shows to best advantage the figure held up through most of Western culture as the thinking human being: Socrates at his wiliest defending his own life. Plato's dialogues, most of which feature Socrates confounding sophists and other Greek leaders on points of philosophy, cover just about every issue that has absorbed philosophers ever since. The *Apology* is unique among the dialogues, first because Socrates is not primarily drawing an opponent into contradictions (though he can't help himself), and second, because he talks at great length about himself.

The *Crito* is a sequel to the trial, in Socrates' prison cell. He is tempted by his friend to escape with his life. Socrates' answer is that he cannot escape his life or its meaning.

Dangerous book—Spiegelberg: "[The] *Apology*, taken seriously and read imaginatively, is anything but a safe bookshelf classic."

All things debated—Emerson: "Out of Plato come all things that are still written and debated among men of thought."

What is an apology?

A defense—West: "An 'apology' is a speech of defense against an accusation of injustice. The word *apo-logia* itself denotes a 'speaking-away,' an explanatory discourse intended to repulse a charge against oneself."

Many apologies—Stone: "There were, as we know from scattered references, many ancient apologies of Socrates beside those of Plato and Xenophon. ...All but one of them, an *Apology* written by Libanius in the fourth century CE, were lost....Libanius wrote an *Apology* in which Socrates speaks like a modern civil libertarian."

Who was Socrates?

Socrates was born about 470 BCE. His father Sophroniscus may have been a sculptor. His mother Phaenarete was a midwife. Socrates was an associate or disciple of Archelaus, who followed the teachings of Anaxagoras—physical philosophy or cosmology—which sought to answer questions about the nature of the world. Socrates was intimate with the friends of Pericles: Aspasia, Alcibiades, Callias, Axiochus. Socrates knew astronomy and geometry well. He served as hoplite in the military campaigns of Samos (441–440 BCE), Potidaea (432–430), Delium (424), and Amphipolis (422?); he was noted for stamina and selfless courage. Sometimes he stood rapt in thought for as long as 24 hours. When he did develop his Socratic method, he always denied having disciples or a school. His deep consideration for the qualities of a good citizen changed the focus of Greek philosophy from cosmology to ethics and principles of living.

Middle class family—Winspear: "Socrates was born around the year 470 BCE. His mother, Phaenarete, is mentioned as a skilled midwife.... According to the long accepted tradition, his father, Sophroniscus, was a craftsman who exercised his art in sculpturing and stone cutting."

Meager income—Stone: "How did Socrates earn his bread? He had a wife and three sons to support. He lived to the age of seventy. But he never seems to have had a job or practiced a trade. His days were spent in leisure, talking. Socrates derided the Sophists for taking payment from their pupils. He prided himself on never asking a fee from his own disciples. How did he support his family?...The answer seems to be that he lived on a small in heritance left him by his father, who did well at his trade of stone-cutter. The income seems to have been meager."

Sculptures on the Acropolis—Winspear: "Pausanias and Diogenes Laertius speak of the Three Graces on the Acropolis as the work of Socrates himself.... In Greek antiquity the artist was not regarded with the same respect that the modern age accords him[/her]."

Two wives—Winspear: "On the question of Socrates' two wives the evidence seems to me overwhelming that there were two ladies in his life.... He seems to have married a woman of his own class, Xanthippe, at an early age. Later he married a lady of patrician family, one Myrto, the great-granddaughter of Aristides the Just.... We may reasonably conclude that Socrates made his second marriage when he was in his late forties [425 BCE]."

Social status—Stone: "The clearest indication of his own social status is given by his military service. He did not fight in the cavalry with aristocrats like Alcibiades. Nor was he enlisted with the poor in the light-armed infantry or at the oars of the navy Socrates fought as a hoplite, a heavy-armed foot soldier. An Athenian had to provide his own military equipment. Only the middle class of craftsmen and merchants could afford the heavy armor of the hoplite."

Three children—Grant: At the time of his death he had one grown-up son, Lamprocles, and two infants."

Death—Socrates died in 399 BCE from hemlock, after sentence of death was passed by Athenian assembly, and after the sacred ship from Delos returned.

Asks questions—Winspear: "Socrates is the philosopher who asks questions to which he does not know the answers. His wisdom consists of an awareness of ignorance."

Who was Plato?

Family—Plato, a nickname meaning wide or flat, was given to a boy named Aristocles, who was born in Athens in 427 BCE. His family was descended from kings, and they maintained an aristocratic tradition. Plato's father was Ariston, his mother Perictione. When Ariston died, Perictione married her uncle Pyrilampes, who was a supporter of Pericles, and who probably brought up Plato.

Political relatives—Perictione's brother, Plato's uncle, was Charmides, her cousin was Critias—both were deeply involved in the pro-Spartan oligarchic Terror of 404, in which 1,500 citizens were rounded up and executed. Plato early had political ambitions, but he had held back from running for public office, and was not directly implicated when the oligarchs showed their hand.

No plays or poetry—Stone: "One of Plato's ancient biographers, Olympiodorus, tells us that Plato originally wanted to be a playwright, a tragic or a comic poet. [but] ... when Plato met Socrates and fell under the older man's spell, he burnt his efforts at tragic poetry and turned instead to philosophy."

No military service—Plato was of an age for military service during the long Peloponnesian War, but we have no record of his having served as a soldier against Sparta.

No wife—In the various biographies of Plato, no mention is made of a wife.

Followed Socrates—He joined the circle of youths who followed Socrates, and wrote many dialogues, in more than twenty of which Socrates is the main character. Plato was 28 years old when the trial of Socrates was held in 399 BCE. Five years afterward he wrote the *Apology*.

Plato was at the trial—Stone: "Plato, unlike Xenophon, was present at the trial of Socrates, as we know from the *Apology*, but seems to have fled the city before the execution."

Travels—After Socrates was condemned to death, Plato and other supporters fled to Megara. Plato then traveled to the rest of Greece, Egypt, Italy and Sicily—all were sites of Greek colonies or trading outposts.

Colleague, not follower–Spiegelberg: "[Plato] never called [Socrates] his teacher or master but only his older friend and companion...[He] never put him on as high a pedestal as the merely defending and adoring Xenophon had done."

The Academy–Around 387 BCE Plato founded the Academy for teaching systematic philosophy, which became a rival institution to the school of Isocrates.

Sicily experiment–In 367, he was tutor to Dionysius II in Sicily, a failed experiment. He revisited Sicily in 361, and failed again to produce a philosopher-king.

Why did Plato write the Apology?

Radical movement–Winspear: "The intellectual argument was closely bound up with the political argument. Anaxagoras, Phidias, Euripides, Socrates, all excited the anger of the oligarchs because their thinking and their creative achievements represented the intellectual and artistic side of the radical, or democratic movement. ... The great sophists were chiefly interested in the problem of justice.... In sophistic philosophy the individual becomes an independent unit."

Dialogues as teasers–A.E. Taylor: "It can hardly be doubted that [Plato] regarded his dialogues as intended in the main to interest an educated outside world in the more serious and arduous labours of his 'school.' "

Winspear: "There was nothing in ancient Athens at all analogous to the modern industrial proletariat. Sophroniscus was an artisan and as such a member of the dynamic, rising, radical class of fifth-century Athens. The attitude of patrician Athenians to this group ... Plato fully shared.... It was important for Plato and Xenophon to ignore or conceal his artisan past."

Who else wrote firsthand about Socrates?

Several authors–Isocrates intimates that a number of pieces of Socratic literature had been written; today we have Xenophon's dialogues, Plato's, and considerable fragments of dialogues by Aeschines, and a few fragments from Antisthenes. We also know about Polycrates' *Accusation of Socrates* (between 394 and 388 BCE) put in the mouth of Anytus, and a dialogue by Lysias of Socrates' reply, but these, and other dialogues that are quoted or referred to, have not survived.

Various speeches of Socrates–Speeches of Socrates have been ascribed to Plato, Xenophon (or pseudo-Xenophon), Lysias, Theodectes, Demetrius of Phalerum, Zeno of Sidon, Plutarch, Theo of Antioch, Libanius.

Xenophon in Asia—Xenophon did not return from Asia until 394 BCE., and therefore could not have access to eyewitness accounts until five years after the trial. Xenophon's return coincided with Plato's publication of his *Apology of Socrates*.

Is Plato's text accurate?

Hackforth lists the experts who think the *Apology* is reasonably accurate:

> Ernst August Horneffer
> John Burnet (1924)
> Alfred Edward Taylor (1926)
> Coleman Phillipson (1928)

and experts who think Plato modified the truth:

> Ivo Bruns (1896)
> Ulrich von Wilamowitz-Möllendorff (1920)

and experts who think Plato's account is largely fictional: ·

> Martin von Schanz (1893)
> Gilbert Murray (1897)
> Robert von Pöhlmann (1906)
> Max Pohlenz (1913)
> John Bagnall Bury (1927) "epilogue...imagined
>   by Plato"
> E. Wolff (1929)

Unrealistic exchange—Hackforth: "Why ... did Plato write these pages [the interrogation of Meletus]? I think there were two reasons: first, he felt that no picture of Socrates could be adequate which did not contain an example of his dialectical ability.... Secondly, there is reason to believe that Plato disliked and despised Meletus.... Xenophon's *Apology* also contains a short passage in which Socrates directly interrogates Meletus."

Not objective—Plato definitely wrote the *Apology* in the spirit of justifying or resurrecting the reputation of Socrates, some five years after the event. The issue of Socrates' death remained a political football for years afterward, as we know by references to the many dialogues or speeches by accusers and accused.

Not a transcription—This dialogue by Plato, although it is in the form of a verbatim court report, is definitely a literary production. Nothing in it is careless; it is extremely persuasive.

Reportage standards—At the time Plato wrote, the Greeks hadn't invented biography. Plato's model for literary truthfulness no doubt stemmed directly from Thucydides who, in his writing of history, invented speeches suitable to historic occasions, to put in the mouths of the historical figures. This practice was in a long Greek tradition: writing poems in praise of athletes or persons. The same tradition continues today in historical fiction, where authors regularly recreate dialogue that couldn't possibly have been overheard; likewise in our day, Hollywood films and TV dramatizations present imaginative recreations or reconstructions of what might have happened.

Character descriptions—Hackforth: "About three-quarters of the *Apology* is in reported speech.... We shall be justified in regarding all this as the author's own invention.... But in terming this 'invention' I ... mean that the composition is of that type where the primary aim is not to record facts but to describe a character, or rather certain aspects of a character."

The first speech—Hackforth: "I believe Plato to have reproduced the real speech with considerable fidelity."

Interrogation of Meletus—Hackforth: "From that point onward to the end of the first speech invention prevailed over reproduction."

End of first speech—Hackforth: "At the necessary cost of obliterating Socrates' defence against the second part of the indictment, he was at once compelled and enabled to describe his master as he saw him, and to give to his readers for all time the splendid pages which close the first speech."

The exordium—Hackforth: "I find no reason to doubt, and some to believe, that it is very much what Socrates said."

The second and third speeches—Hackforth: "The second speech and the third ... seem to me much closer to reality than the section we have been considering."

True to life—Hackforth: "My own belief is that the Socrates of the *Apology* is true to life, and that any evidence which conflicts with it must be rejected."

What did Socrates' contemporaries say?

Teacher of Critias, an oligarch—Aeschines [in 345 BCE]: "[The Athenians] put to death Socrates the sophist ... because he was shown to have been the teacher of Critias, one of the Thirty who put down the democracy."

Anytus on the sophists—Taylor: "[In Plato's *Meno*] Anytus assures us vehemently that the sophists, who claim to be ...professionals [of virtue], are mischievous impostors."

Aristippus—Spiegelberg: "There is very little direct information about the minor Socratic schools like the Cynics and Cyrenaics. But it is apparent that the founder of hedonism, Aristippus, admired him."

Epicurus—Spiegelberg: "[Epicurus gives Socrates a] polite, telling silence."

Zeno of Sidon—Spiegelberg: "[The Epicurean Zeno of Sidon called him a] crude buffoon of the Athenian streets."

The Skeptics—Spiegelberg: "The early Skeptics, judging from Timon's lampoon and Arcesilaus' stricture, objected to his inconsistent skepticism."

Zeno and the Stoics—Spiegelberg: "The founder, Zeno of Citium, upon reading the second book of Xenophon's *Memorabilia* [of Socrates], was looking for followers of Socrates. It was apparently in Hellenized Rome that Socrates found a much stronger following .... To the later Stoics he became actually the model human being."

Julian the Apostate—Spiegelberg: "The apostate emperor Julian, in his belated attempt to revive paganism, plays him off as a hero even against more famous secular competitors."

Christians pro and con—Spiegelberg: "St. Justin Martyr [was] from the very start his chief advocate among Christians, and Origen ... see[s] in Socrates a peacemaker, a fellow martyr, and even a Christian before Christ. Simultaneously, however, there is the anti-Socratism of Tertullian, Lactantius, and Chrysostom, who cannot admit the relevance and adequacy of reason in matters of faith.... Only the Platonist St. Augustine approached Socrates in a more objective manner and took exception merely to his hostility to metaphysics."

Why is this trial taking place now?

Why now? Socrates was seventy years old, and amnesty had been declared after the war.

A conspiracy—At least one of his accusers, Anytus, apparently believed that Socrates was part of an ongoing conspiracy to bring down the government of Athens.

The amnesty—Stone: "The amnesty that followed the overthrow of the Thirty did not wipe out the stigma on those who had taken no part in the resistance.... Socrates was protected by the amnesty, too. He could not be prosecuted for anything he had said or done before the restoration of the democracy.... Had the indictment covered these earlier activities, it would have been attacked at the trial as a blatant violation of the amnesty.... This indictment, to be valid, could cover only the activities or teachings of Socrates in the four years between the overthrow of the Thirty and the trial."

Witch hunt trials—Dodds: "About 432 BCE or a year or two later, disbelief in the supernatural and the teaching of astronomy were made indictable offenses. The next thirty-odd years witnessed a series of heresy trials.... The victims included most of the leaders of progressive thought at Athens—Anaxagoras, Diagoras, Socrates, almost certainly Protagoras also, and possibly Euripides."

No witch hunt—Stone: "I believe the evidence for all this is belated and dubious.... No 'evidence' of a witch-hunt appears any earlier than in writers of the Roman era, principally Plutarch, who wrote about five centuries after Socrates."

New gods—Hackforth: "The new gods whom he was accused of introducing were the mystic divinities of Pythagorean sects—the militant protective deities of international conservatism. It should be clear, too, that this suspicion in the minds of Athenians could not have been of long standing. It could, in no case, have dated back earlier than about 415, and probably did not become acute until after 406. In the *Apology*, Socrates takes great pains to confuse the issue ... attempting to push the distrust back much earlier in time."

Nature of the trial—Winspear: "The setting of the trial, to begin with, was extremely interesting. The democracy, having restored itself and balanced the rather precarious political position, felt it necessary to deal with the problem of Socrates. Three men came forward as his accusers: Meletus for the poets, Anytus for the craftsmen and political leaders, and Lycon for the rhetoricians. These three groups represent the intellectual as well as the practical leadership of the democracy.... The democracy was almost incredibly tolerant toward the men who attempted to destroy it. The only intelligible motive we can ascribe to the democrats arose out of a perfectly sober estimate of the danger both past and present represented by Socrates."

What was the larger political picture?

War with Sparta—The Peloponnesian War between the Delian League (some called it the Athenian empire) and Sparta and its allies had been going on for four years and would last until Plato was 23 years old. The eventual defeat of Athens caused a great deal of soul-searching among Athenians, who had reached their golden age under Pericles, who had died just before Plato was born.

Socrates unfair to Sophists—Stone: "The antagonism between Socrates and the Sophists, as portrayed in Xenophon and Plato, has blackened their name.... There is a strong element of class prejudice in the Socratic animosity toward the Sophists. They were teachers who found their market in democratic cities like Athens among a rising middle class of well-to-do craftsmen and traders. ... Elementary education for all citizens was achieved early in Athens, at least a century before Socrates, and literacy seems to have been widespread. This reflected the rise of democracy. But the higher education remained the monopoly of the aristocracy until the Sophists came along. They provoked upper-class antagonism by teaching the arts of rhetoric."

A decade of earthquakes—Stone: "How is it that no one filed a complaint against [Socrates] until he was seventy? ... The answer, I believe, lies in three political 'earthquakes' that occurred in little more than a decade before the trial, shaking the city's sense of internal security and making its citizens apprehensive.... In 411 BCE and again in 404, disaffected elements in connivance with the Spartan enemy overthrew the democracy, set up dictatorships, and initiated a reign of terror. In 401 BCE, only two years before the trial, they were about to try again. The type of rich young men prominent in the entourage of Socrates played a leading role in all three civic convulsions.... The 'Socratified' youth of [Aristophanes'] *The Birds* with their Spartan-style clubs no longer looked dashing and cute. They had become the storm troopers with which the Four Hundred in 411 and the Thirty in 404 terrorized the city. In the elegant and seductive phrases of his *Apology*, Plato does not allow these political events to obtrude on the reader, though they were fresh in the memories of the judges."

Spartan lackeys—Stone: "The dictatorship of the Thirty, as the narrow oligarchy that replaced the assembly in 404 was called, was set up with the connivance of the Spartans in the wake of their victory over Athens in the Peloponnesian war. Among the disaffected aristocrats who served as tools of the Spartan victors

... were Critias and Charmides.... Both were relatives of Plato's, the former a first cousin, the latter his uncle."

Secret societies—Burnet: "[The synomosias] were originally devised to secure the election to office of members of the oligarchical party and their acquittal when put on trial, and ... played so great a part in the revolutions at the end of the fifth century BCE."

Enemies of democracy—Gomme: "Only enemies of democracy needed secret organizations."

Restricted vote—Women in Athens had no vote, nor did slaves, of whom in wartime there were a considerable number.

War lost—In 404 BCE, Athens lost its war with Sparta, and many Athenian citizens were disillusioned with their democratic form of government.

What were the charges against Socrates?

Why Socrates?—Stone: "Here a crucial question arises which is neither raised nor answered in Plato's *Apology*. Why should a reputation for wisdom get a man into trouble in a city like Athens, a city to which philosophers flocked from all over Greece and were not only welcomed but richly rewarded as teachers and popular lecturers? ... The answer seems to be that Socrates used his special kind of 'wisdom'—his *sophia* or skill as a logician and philosopher—for a special political purpose: to make all the leading men of the city appear to be ignorant fools.... He thus undermined the *polis*, defamed the men on whom it depended, and alienated the youth."

Pythagorean link—Hackforth: "A.E. Taylor has discussed the nature of the real charge, proving beyond question that the accusation was based on Socrates' known affinity for the Pythagorean sects.... There is the unquestionable fact of a contact between Socrates and a number of men who can be directly linked to the Pythagorean cults. Some of their names appear in the Platonic dialogues."

Insults not a crime—Stone: "I do not wish to imply that Socrates was finally brought to trial for casting aspersions on Athenian statesmen. Insulting them was not a crime in Athens. It was a popular sport. The comic poets—who played something of the same role in Athens as independent journalists in our world—did it all the time, to the intense enjoyment of the Athenians. Socrates' real offense lay in his gross oversimplifications—in the simplistic philosophical premises from which he leveled his attacks on the city, its leaders, and the democracy."

Polycrates' pamphlet—Stone: "Xenophon [in the *Memorabilia*] ...

refs to the charges brought against Socrates by an 'accuser,' whom he does not identify. But modern scholars long ago decided that this reference is not to a prosecutor at the actual trial but to a lost pamphlet by a prodemocratic writer named Polycrates, which was published soon after the trial was over."

Personal animosity of Anytus—Stone: "Something other than politics seems to have aggravated relations between Anytus and Socrates, a disagreement over the education of Anytus' son.... It appears that there was a rivalry between Socrates and Anytus for the younger man's devotion. 'At one time,' Socrates reveals in Xenophon's *Apology*, ' I had a brief association with the son of Anytus, and I thought him not lacking in firmness of spirit.' ... Anytus was not unreasonable in withdrawing his son from Socratic tutelage."

The accusers—Stone: "Of the three accusers of Socrates, the only one prominent in Athens was Anytus. The other two, Meletus and Lycon, were obscure men of whom little is known beyond what Socrates himself tells us of them in the *Apology*.... Yet in the *Apology* we hear only from Meletus, who proves a bit dim-witted and an easy pushover for Socrates."

Critias an invisible witness—Stone: "We never hear from Anytus in the *Apology*, and Critias is never mentioned, but they are contrapuntal figures behind the trial. Critias, though dead, was in a sense the chief witness for the prosecution.... The high repute of Anytus and the bad repute of Critias were the chief obstacles to an acquittal."

Corrupt or lead astray?—Stone: "The word *corrupted* may create a false impression. It sounds to modern ears like the allegation of a homosexual offense. But pederasty—an erotic attachment between a man and a beardless youth—was socially respectable in classical Greece.... The verb used in the indictment—διαπητηειρειν—can mean destroy, corrupt, seduce, or lead astray.... Plato uses ... the same Greek word to mean leading the youth astray politically. The fragments of Polycrates in Xenophon show us that the word had the same meaning in the indictment of Socrates."

Anytus a moderate—Stone: "The most influential of the three accusers of Socrates at his trial—a man named Anytus—was a lieutenant of Theramenes [leader of the moderate oligarchical party]. Anytus was one of the middle-class moderates who fled Athens after the execution of Theramenes, joined the democrats in the exiled opposition, and became one of the generals who led the coalition of moderates and democrats which overthrew the Thirty and restored the democracy. Anytus must have held it against Socrates that he had joined neither the moderates nor the democrats in opposition to the Thirty."

Socrates insulted Anytus—Stone: "Anytus was a master tanner. It seems from Xenophon's *Apology* that Socrates had insulted him by speaking disdainfully of Anytus' vulgar occupation and criticizing him for bringing up his own son in the same vulgar occupation."

Accusation according to Xenophon—Stone: "According to Xenophon 'his accuser' said Socrates 'taught his companions' to look down upon the laws of Athens, led them 'to despise the established constitution and made them violent,' that is, ready to use force to overthrow it. The accuser cited Critias and Alcibiades as the foremost examples of this corrupted youth and said that 'none wrought so many evils to the state.' Critias as the leading figure in the dictatorship of the Thirty 'bore the palm for greed and violence,' while Alcibiades under the democracy 'exceeded all in licentiousness and insolence.' "

Gods: Peitho, Zeus Agoraios, Demos—Stone: "[In] the *Oresteia* [of Aeschylus], Athena, the Olympian and universal Greek Goddess, pays tribute for her victory over the Furies to two 'gods of the city' peculiar to Athens. They are Peitho, or persuasion personified as a goddess, and the Zeus Agoraios, or the Zeus of the assembly, the tutelary divinity of its free debates. They embodied the democratic institutions of Athens.... In [*The Frogs*] Aristophanes staged a debate between Aeschylus and Euripides ... [who] hurl one-line quotations at each other about Persuasion [Peitho] from their plays.... The two greatest masters of fourth-century oratory—Demosthenes and Isocrates—also list Peitho among 'the gods of the city' and refer to annual sacrifices in her honor.... She was commemorated in sculpture by Praxiteles and Pheidias.... Today in the colonnade of the Agora Museum in Athens there is a relief showing Democracy crowning Demos {the People]—an elderly bearded man seated on a throne.... There are two other passages in Pausanias about a deified Demos in Attica."

Synomosias—Stone: "In 411 and 404 democracy was not overthrown by a popular revulsion but by a handful of conspirators.... It is against this background that we can better understand a curious denial entered by Socrates in Plato's *Apology*. There he says that all his life long he had avoided taking part in synomosias. This is translated as 'plots' in the Loeb, and in Jowett. But the word ...

derives from a Greek verb that means to take an oath together. It was applied to the more or less secret clubs or conspiracies in which aristocrats bound themselves by oath to help each other and to work against the democracy.... There is no reason to doubt Socrates' denial of membership. But ... Socrates' denial that he himself had ever joined a synomosia is the only point in the *Apology* where he touches—though ever so lightly—on what I believe to have been the real political issues behind his trial."

How did Socrates defend himself?

No defense at all—Hackforth: "It is even very doubtful whether Socrates made any defense at all. We are inclined to believe that Dr. H. Gomperz and Prof. W.A. Oldfather have proved conclusively that he did not.... By way of direct evidence, there is the explicit statement of Maximus of Tyre that Socrates gave no defense for himself, but that he 'kept silence without faltering.' ... The three speeches that have survived differ so widely both in content and manner that it is impossible to believe that they go back to one original."

Stone's proposal for a defense—Stone (as Socrates): "Let me be frank. I do not believe in your so-called freedom of speech, but you do. I believe the opinions of ordinary men are only δοξα—beliefs without substance, pale shadows of reality, not to be taken seriously, and only likely to lead a city astray. I think it absurd to encourage the free utterance of unfounded or irrational opinions, or to base civic policy on a count of heads, like cabbages. Hence I do not believe in democracy. but you do. This is your test, not mine."

Words for free speech—Stone: "Obviously Athenians enjoyed free speech. But did they think of it as a basic principle of government, as we do? ... I found no less than four [Greek] words for freedom of speech.... I found that no other people in history prized free speech more than the Greeks, and this was especially true of the Athenians.... With the struggle for democracy, more than two hundred compounds containing the word ισος for equal were added to the language.... Two ... were words for the right of free speech, isegoria and isologia.... Latin had no word for ισεγορια. Roman law had no use for it.... The *Suppliant Maidens* of Aeschylus ... introduces us to a compound term for free speech made up of two roots—ελευτηερος (free) and στομος (mouth).... A fourth Greek word for freedom of speech—παρρηεσια—is one of [Euripides'] favorite themes.... It is hard to find even a mention of the four words for freedom of speech in Socrates and his followers. It is as if they found even the terms for free speech distasteful. Of the four, only one, παρρηεσια, appears in the Platonic dialogues."

Plea of a partisan—Winspear: "Viewed from this point of view we read the *Apology of Socrates* in a very different light. We are so used to thinking of the work as the high-minded apologia of the philosophic man, remote from mundane things, high above politics and politicial striving, that it is difficult to think of it as the extremely adroit and facile plea of a partisan."

No reconciliation—Stone: "I believe there never would have been a trial had he, too, demonstrated his own reconciliation with the democracy, had he paid some tribute—as Xenophon did—to the magnanimity of the majority in the peace settlement. Had any such change in his attitude taken place, he would have allayed fear that a new crop of 'Socratified' and alienated youth might emerge from his following to unleash civil war again within the city. But there is no evidence, either in Plato or Xenophon, of any such change in Socrates after the overthrow of the Thirty. Socrates resumed his antidemocratic and antipolitical teachings."

Martyr of free speech—Stone: "[Socrates] was the first martyr of free speech and free thought. If he had conducted his defense as a free speech case, and invoked the basic traditions of his city, he might easily, I believe, have shifted the troubled jury in his favor. Unfortunately Socrates never invoked the principle of free speech. Perhaps one reason he held back from that line of defense is because his victory would also have been a victory for the democratic principles he scorned. An acquittal would have vindicated Athens."

Socrates in Athens during the violence—Burnet: "Observe that Socrates himself remained in Athens.... It was a good deal more imprudent to remind the judges of that than it was advantageous to recall the democratic opinions of Chaerephon."

Victim of repression—Stone: "We are still left, however, with a puzzling question: Why doesn't Plato in his *Apology* have Socrates cite the law against the teaching of the τεχηνε λογον [art of reasoned discourse discussed in Xenophon's *Apology*] to prove that he was himself a victim of repression by the Thirty?"

No rebuttals—Stone: "Plainly none of these passages contains any rebuttal of the specific points which must have been made in the speeches for the prosecution.... Why then has Plato omitted this part of Socrates' defence?"

Imperative of the oracle—Stone: "The sole source of the difficulty is the attachment of an imperative to the interpretation of the oracle which Plato makes Socrates give. The attachment of that imperative I believe to be Plato's own doing: and his motive, I think, was a perfectly simple and a perfectly honest motive: he wanted to explain to himself and others why Socrates had believed himself to be sent by God to serve his people. Socrates had not given any explanation at the trial, and probably not at any time: why not? Because there was no explanation to give: he just believed it to be so."

Relationship to the oracle—Winspear: "Socrates states unambiguously that at the beginning of his labors he was trying to refute the oracle. After he began his examinations, his attitude toward the oracle became unclear. However, by the end of the examinations, Socrates becomes the oracle's champion and spokesman."

Misleading charges—In his account, Xenophon shows Socrates admitting each fact, but showing how misleading or malicious inferences were made from them.

What is the "Socratic problem"?

Sudden conversion—Winspear: "Socrates went through a philosophical conversion; this conversion was a turning-away from materialism and a concept of material causation to idealism and a belief in teleological causation.... This new way of thinking is represented by Plato as a sudden change."

Socrates becomes two symbols—Hackforth: "Socrates, then, within the space of a few years from the trial, had become a symbol around which the co-related intellectual and political battle of Athenian and Greek factions was raging.... The whole effort of the conservative faction was to lift Socrates above the struggle of contending factions and make him a symbol of certain eternal and absolute moral and religious ideas. The aim of the democrats, on the other hand, was to keep the argument on a strictly political level.... In this way two distinct conceptions of Socrates developed."

Aristophanes vs. Plato—Winspear: "The contradiction between the Aristophanic representation and the Platonic idealization of [Socrates] is inescapable.... The more one examines the historical Socrates, the more uncertain one becomes of his value as a moral example."

Socrates followed Archelaus—Winspear: "Socrates evidently spent many years in close association with Archelaus and was probably a member of his school."

Archelaus on ethics—Winspear: "[According to Diogenes,] Archelaus united his materialistic and evolutionary theories with a thoroughly sophistic view of ethics and human institutions. 'The just and the base are not so by nature but rather by convention.' "

Changed when independent—Winspear: "In the period from 432 to 423 Socrates seems to have gone through the social and intellectual transition which marked the turning point of his life.... It seems very probable that Socrates at this period was independently wealthier than at any other time in his life."

Two stages—Winspear: "In Plato's *Phaedo* ... Socrates discourses ... 'When I was young,' he says, 'I had a wondrous desire for the wisdom that they call inquiry about nature.' He wanted to learn 'the causes of each thing: why each thing comes into being, why it perishes, and why it is.' ... He concluded that he could not thereby obtain the knowledge he desired, since the direct observation of things did not lead him to their causes. So he turned away from the investigation of beings 'in deed,' that is, in their visible manifestations, to their investigation 'in speeches.' 'It seemed to me that I should take refuge in speeches [λογοι] and consider in them the truth about the beings.' ... According to this account, Socrates' career had two stages, one devoted to the inquiry about nature, and the other to the 'refuge in speeches.' ... This later inquiry, wherein he pressed the meaning of ordinary speech to the very limit, caused him to be easily confused with mere verbal quibblers. His relentless pursuit of the implications of men's opinions often led to blatantly paradoxical conclusions."

Two views of Socrates—Winspear: "The apparent contradiction between the Platonic-Xenophontic and the Aristophanic accounts has given rise to a much-discussed controversy among classical philologists over the so-called Socratic problem. Much elaborate speculation and conjecture has been propounded to explain the differences, and the dominant opinion maintains that 'Aristophanes attaches to Socrates the characteristics which belonged to the sophists in general but did not belong to Socrates.' "

A continuing argument—Spiegelberg: "These opinions [of critics through the ages] began to form a coherent story. Socrates turned out to be the persistent theme of a continuing argument in which nearly all the major figures in the history of ideas since Socrates' days had taken part."

Why did Socrates attack the early accusers first?

Different accusations—Hackforth: "He deliberately confounds two quite separate things; the accusations that Aristophanes had made against him—based on the intellectual interests of his early manhood—with the distrust that had arisen much later.... The rest of the Apology is in the same way an essay in persuasion."

Pro-Spartanism in Aristophanes' account—Stone: "It is significant that in the *Apology*, where Socrates blames the prejudice against him on the comic poets, he refers only to *The Clouds* of Aristophanes. He makes no reference to the pro-Spartanism alleged in *The Birds*. That play has a direct bearing on the charge in Socrates' indictment that he subverted the loyalty of the youth to Athens. *The Birds* supported that charge when it described the pro-Spartan "laconomaniac" youth of Athens as "Socratified." ... The foremost example of those "Socratified' malcontents was Plato himself. In the fourth century BCE he carried on the same intellectual assault against Athenian freedom and democracy that his master had launched in the fifth."

Disrespect to gods widespread—Stone: "There is no record of anyone ever having been prosecuted in Athens because of what was said about him by comic poets. If their jokes had been taken seriously, most of the city's statesmen would have ended up in jail.... As for not believing in gods, the Athenians were accustomed to hearing the gods treated disrespectfully in both the comic and the tragic theater. For two centuries before Socrates, the philsophers had been laying the foundations of natural science and metaphysical inquiry.... In the process the ancient gods were not so much dethroned as demoted and bypassed. They were reduced to venerable fables or metaphorical personifications of natural forces and abstract ideas.... Polytheism was, by its very pluralistic nature, roomy and tolerant, open to new gods and new views of old ones.... Atheism was little known and difficult for a pagan to grasp because [s/]he saw divinity all about him[/her], not just on Olympus but in the hearth and the boundary stone.... One could in the same city and the same century worship Zeus as a promiscuous old rake, henpecked and cuckolded by Juno, or as Justice deified."

Socrates an active participant—Magalhaes-Vilhena: "Socrates is not the pure contemplative dreamer ... but an active participant in the political and social and ideological quarrels of the city state and one whose participation was conscious."

The beauty of truth—Winspear: "Socrates seems to reject the καλον, the beautiful or noble, as the basis of right speech and action. He opposes here a long Greek tradition, which used the term καλον as high praise for an outstanding man's appearance and deeds.... Yet Socrates does not simply abandon nobility, for he also calls his accusers' speech shameful or ugly (αισχηρον) ...He thereby propounds a standard of beauty that distinguishes the superficial beauty of adornment and order from the genuine beauty of truth.... Socrates [makes the] unexpected assertion that '[the virtue] of an orator is to speak the truth.' "

Criminal intellect—Winspear: "For the first accusers, his intellectual life is the source of his crimes."

Did the Athenians convict Socrates unjustly?

Wanted to be convicted—Stone: "Why was Socrates so surprised by the close vote for conviction? ... Xenophon says Socrates wanted to be convicted and did his best to antagonize the jury.... He did not wish to charm them. The tone he adopted in his address to the jury was offensively boastful and arrogant.... Xenophon ... based his account on what he was told later by Hermogenes, one of Socrates' closest disiciples."

Offensive attitude—Burnet: "We have no means of checking this, but a considerable turnover of votes [for death penalty] would not be surprising in view of the attitude taken up by Socrates."

Arrogance of Socrates—Winspear: "The unpersuasiveness of Socrates' speech ... lies particularly in its arrogant, insulting attitude toward the jury of Athenian citizens.... Since we are not part of the jury he treats so rudely, we easily imagine, as human beings are wont to do, that we are quite superior to the vulgar men chastised by Socrates."

Democratic sense of justice—Stone: "Aristotle recognized that the very concept of 'justice,' instead of being something only the rare few could achieve, sprang from deep roots in common human experience and in [hu]man's very nature as a 'political animal.' So the oath taken by the Athenian jurors—to act 'justly"—implied that they had an innate sense of justice.... This common stock of 'civic virtue' was the basis on which Athens practiced democracy and Aristotle formulated equity." The negative dialectic of Socrates—if the city had taken it seriously—would have made equity and democracy impossible. His identification of virtue with an unattainable knowledge stripped common [hu]men of hope and denied their capacity to govern themselves."

Threat to democracy—The Athenian assembly acted lawfully, and in response to what some perceived as a threat to the democratic principles upon which the Athenian state rested, at a time when its very existence was being called into question from extreme elements on the political right and the left. The aristocratic party preferred at least oligarchy, if not tyrant rulership.

What was the public reaction after the trial?

No revulsion—Stone: "I, too, believe that there should have been a revulsion against the verdict that condemned Socrates. But there is no sign of it in the surviving literature of the century after his death. Socrates did not become a cult figure outside the Platonic academy until long after his death."

Athenian repentance—Diodorus and Diogenes Laertius both tell stories relating to Athenian repentance for the death of Socrates.

Flood of argument—Hackforth: "Around the figure of Socrates a veritable literary warfare developed. His friends and supporters poured forth a flood of argument, rhetoric, direct and indirect defense. As part of this systematic campaign, we can certainly include the *Gorgias* of Plato, the *Meno* of Plato, the *Apology* of Lysias, the *Memorabilia* of Xenophon, the *Apology* of Xenophon (or pseudo-Xenophon) as well as the famous *Platonic Apology*. Nor were his opponents silent; in the year 393 or shortly after, the sophist and pamphleteer Polycrates published an attack on Socrates which purported to convey the case for the prosecution at the trial."

Keen discussion—Winspear: "Modern scholars ... have often suggested that the trial and its sequel became a topic of keen discussion."

Was Socrates singled out?

Meletus accuses another—Meletus is on record as having spoken against Andocides on the same charge of irreligion in the same year.

Strange gods—Hackforth: "The *Apology* contains no reply, or at least no formal and direct reply, to the charge of introducing καινα δαιμονια [strange gods].... It aims at proving, not that Socrates did not introduce strange gods, but that he believed in gods."

Not a good citizen—Stone: "By these standards [of citizen participation required by Solon], Socrates was not a good citizen. He did his duty as a soldier, and acquitted himself bravely. But it is extraordinary that so prominent an Athenian managed in his seventy years to take almost no part at all in civic affairs."

What do moderns say about Socrates?

Ficino and Erasmus–Spiegelberg: "Marsilio Ficino, head of the new Florentine Academy rediscovered the hero of the *Apology* and drew a dangerously close parallel between his fate and Jesus' Passion. But it was Erasmus' near-canonization of the pagan sage which caused the real scandal."

The Deists–Spiegelberg: "It is the eighteenth century which shows Socratism at its peak. To Shaftesbury's enthusiasm Socrates seems a nearly divine hero, yet human in the most natural manner. He also becomes, as it were, the patron saint of the Deists, beginning with John Locke and Anthony Collins and ending by inspiring such strange projects as John Toland's Socratic Society."

The French–Spiegelberg: "Voltaire sees him as the greatest sage... Diderot, the moving spirit of the *Encyclopédie*, worships Socrates with an almost touching sentimentalism.... To Montesquieu Socrates is simply an objectionable absolutist à la Plato. But the chief blast comes from the forerunner of romanticism, Rousseau."

Memory, not the man–Spiegelberg: "Socrates was clearly a symbol for issues far bigger than his own person, and in this lies his major significance for posterity.... I would maintain that Socrates' memory–even more than the real Socrates, who remains unknown and unknowable–has been one of the most powerful liberators and defenders of [hu]man, the individual."

Steady anti-Socratism–Spiegelberg: "I had grown tired of the fatuous generalities about his immortal fame, at best relieved by a contemptuous reference to Nietzsche's sacrilegious villainy in attacking it. I had for some time been suspicious of the traditional view, shared even by students of classics, that Socrates had been rehabilitated and canonized by a repenting posterity–a myth which conceals the fact that Socrates has been steadily opposed by anti-Socratism."

Did Socrates have a gospel or teaching?

No consistent philosophy–Most authors conclude that Socrates did not have a consistent philosophy. Plato's system came to be called Idealism, and was later abstracted in Neoplatonism to claim that reality was in ideal models and that the world around us consists of variations on these ideal forms.

Rejects politics–Stone: "Socrates preached and practiced withdrawal from the political life of the city. In Plato's *Apology* he defended this abstention as necessary for 'the perfection' of the soul."

Gadfly needed—Stone: "The Socratic gadfly never seemed to be around when its sting was most needed. Socrates never raised his voice in the assembly when the fateful decisions of his lifetime [the overthrow of the democracy in 411 and again in 404 BCE] were made.... Socrates was aware of the criticism he had provoked by abstention from politics."

Sparta admiration baffling—Stone: "The Socratic admiration for Sparta and Crete...is puzzling. Sparta and Crete were culturally and politically the two most backward regions of ancient Greece. In both, the lands were cultivated by serfs, and the serfs were kept submissive ... by a secret police and a ruling military caste practicing ... apartheid.... Sparta—and probably also Crete—restricted travel abroad by citizens ... to prevent ... the danger of 'spiritual pollution' from foreign ideas."

Was Socrates anti-democratic?

Social anarchy—Hackforth: "What Anytus feared, and regarded as socially dangerous, was in fact the encouragement given by Socrates to young people to examine the principles of their behaviour and their moral judgments; to him and no doubt to many other honest patriots, this was the road to moral licence and social anarchy."

Freemasons—Hackforth: "Taylor suggests that Socrates was the leader of a loose group of aristocratic freemasons with an international character."

Who is elitist?—Plato's *Republic* is decidedly elitist, promoting the idea of philosopher-kings as a ruling class. But Plato is not Socrates.

Herd to be shepherded—Stone: "The various followers of Socrates disagreed, often as violently as modern scholars, as to just what Socrates had taught them.... But on one matter they agreed: They all rejected the polis. They all saw the human community not as a self-governing body of citizens with equal rights but as a herd that required a shepherd or king. They all treated democracy with condescension or contempt."

Intimate with oligarchs—Winspear: "Where was Socrates through all this [political turmoil]? There can be little doubt that he was very intimate with the oligarchical leaders, many of whom he had instructed in the notion that only the good and the wise and the true should rule... His sympathies at such a juncture were with the so-called moderates."

Open criticisms—Winspear: "Neither Socrates nor ... Plato made any attempt to conceal their criticisms of Athenian democracy, its dependence (as they thought) on the whim of the multitude and the caprice of the lot; nor did they conceal their preference for Sparta's more aristocratic, oligarchic and servile organization of society."

Profoundly anti-democratic—Winspear: "The essence of Socrates' teaching was, as we have seen, profoundly anti-democratic, striking at the very theoretical roots on which the democratic way of life (even in a slave-owning democracy) was founded. However much we may excuse Socrates from any responsibility or sanction of the actual violence committed, we must nevertheless realize that the instinct of the democracy was profoundly right when it saw in him the evil genius behind the scene; the *fons et origo malorum* [the fount and origin of evil] the intellectual center from which emanated the very heart and soul of anti-democratic beliefs."

Oligarchic terrorists—Hackforth: "We cannot believe that the uncompromising terrorists, who were responsible for something like fifteen hundred political murders including that of Theramenes, would have hesitated to put the dissident philosopher out of the way."

Conspiracy theory—Hackforth: "Socrates...was suspected of being the head and center of an anti-democratic conspiratorial club. The youth whom he was accused of corrupting were wealthy and patrician young men, like Critias and Alcibiades, whom, it was thought, he had indoctrinated with his own contempt for democracy ... his own conviction that only knowledge and wisdom entitled one to rule."

What is the publishing history of the Apology?

394 BCE—Hackforth places the date of Plato's writing of the *Apology* as not before 394 BCE. Dialogues, speeches and other references to Socrates' death sentence had been published for years.

Bruni's translation—Winspear: "Plato's *Apology*, the *Crito*, and the *Symposium* were inaccessible to the Western world until Leonardo Bruni (1369–1440), the pupil of the Byzantine refugee scholar Manuel Chrysoloras, supplied a Latin translation; only ... Socrates' final speech in the *Apology*, quoted without indication of the source and context in Cicero's *Tusculan Disputations*, were always available.... Nothing of Xenophon's Socrates was known until Cardinal Bessarion (1403-1472) translated the *Memorabilia*."

Nietzsche's attack on Socrates—The great modern attack on

Socrates came in 1872, when Friedrich Nietzsche published *Die Geburt der Tragödie aus dem Geiste der Musik* (*The Birth of Tragedy out of the Spirit of Music*) in 25 sections. Nietzsche attacks Socrates as the force behind rationalism in Euripides, which brought an end to the tragic view of life. Nietzsche wants to bring it back. A new edition, in 1886 was titled *Geburt der Tragödie; oder Griechentum und Pessimismus* (*Birth of Tragedy; or Greekness and Pessimism*) with an introduction "Versuch einer Selbstkritik" (Attempt at Self-Criticism) repudiating the Wagner portions of the book. Both Werner Dannhauser and Walter Kaufmann use the 1886 edition as the basis for their translations.

What is important about the *Crito*?

Trial could have been avoided—Stone: "The same death wish reappears in the *Crito* after the trial and aggravates the disciples.... [Crito] even complains that the case had been allowed to come before the court at all, 'when it might have been avoided.' This cryptic remark still tantalizes us.... Under the [Roman] Republic ... a citizen could evade trial or a death penalty after trial by the option of *exsilium*, or self-exile from the city.... There may have been a similar legal doctrine in Athens."

Praised Sparta and Crete—Burnet: "[This remark in the *Crito* is] pointless unless the 'historical' Socrates had actually praised the laws of Sparta and Crete."

Idealized Sparta—Stone: "Socrates was one of those Athenians who despised democracy and idealized Sparta.... Aristophanes [in *The Birds*] portrays him as the idol of the pro-Spartan malcontents in Athens.... The Socratic infatuation with Sparta is attested in both the Xenophontic and the Platonic portraits of him. The best-known evidence of this is in Plato's *Crito*. There his pro-Spartan bias is referred to in the imaginary dialogue between Socrates and the personified Laws of Athens.... Socrates refuses to be rescued: He will not break the law even to save his life from a verdict he considers unjust."

Law as social contract—Stone: "In this imaginary conversation with the Laws [in the *Crito*], there is set forth the concept of law as a contract between the state and the individual citizen. This is probably the first appearance of the social contract theory in secular literature."

Readiness to die—Stone: "To counter this angry criticism [of Crito], Socrates now offers a new reason.... In an imaginary dialogue with the personified Laws of Athens, he lets himself be convinced that it is his duty to obey the court's verdict and die. This is a unique occasion for Socrates.... The easy surrender is significant.... Scholars are still trying without success to resolve the contradiction between his lifelong nonconformity and his sudden readiness to submit to a verdict that he sees—and so do we—as unjust."

Not welcome in Sparta—Stone: "Apparently the thought of Sparta as a refuge for Socrates never even occurred to Crito and the other devoted disciples who were planning the escape.... The obvious answer, well known in antiquity, would have been embarrassing. Socrates was a philosopher, and philosophers were not welcome in Sparta."

BIBLIOGRAPHY

Aristophanes. *The Birds.* Oxford: Clarendon Press, 1995

_____. *The Clouds.* Cincinnati: American Book, 1915

Aristotle. *Athenian Constitution.* tr. P.J. Rhodes. Harmondsworth: Penguin, 1984

Bruns, Ivo. *Die Verfassungsdebatte bei Herodot.* New York: Arno Press, 1979

Burnet, John. *Euthyphro, Apology of Socrates and Crito.* Oxford: Clarendon Press, 1924

Bury, John Bagnall. *History of Greece to the Death of Alexander.* London: Macmillan, 1902

Dannhauser, Werner J. *Nietzsche's View of Socrates.* Ithaca: Cornell University, 1974.

Diodorus Siculus. *Historical Library of Diodorus the Sicilian.* London: Awnsham & Churchil

Diogenes Laertius. *Lives of the Eminent Philosophers.* Cambridge: Harvard University Press, 1980

Dodds, Eric R. *The Greeks and the Irrational.* Berkeley: University of California Press, 1951

Ferguson, John. *Socrates: A Source Book.* London: Macmillan, 1970. Includes the Libanius *Apology of Socrates.*

Gomme, A.W. with A. Andrewes and K.L. Dover. *A Historical Commentary on Thucydides.* Oxford: Clarendon Press, 1981.

Gomperz, Heinrich. *Platons Selbstbiographie.* Leipzig: de Gruyter, 1928

Grant, Arthur James. *Greece in the Age of Pericles.* London: J. Murray, 1893

Hackforth, Reginald. *The Composition of Plato's Apology.* Cambridge: Cambridge University Press, 1933

Hamilton, Edith and Huntington Cairns. *Plato.* Princeton: Princeton University Press, 1971

Horneffer, Ernst August. *Platonismus und di Gegenwart.* Erfurt: K. Steiner, 1927

Isocrates. *Cinq discours: Eloge d'Helene, Busiris, Contre les sopistes, Sur l'attelage, Contre Callimachos.* Paris: Presses Unibversitaire de France, 1961

Lysias. *Orationes.* Cambridge: Harvard University Press, 1957

Magalhaes-Vilhena, V. de. *Le Probleme de Socrate.* Presses Universitaires de France, 1952

_____. *Socrate et la légende platonicienne.* Paris: Presses Universitaires de France, 1952

Murray, Gilbert. *Greek Studies.* Oxford: Clarendon Press, 1946

Nietzsche, Friedrich. *Birth of Tragedy out of the Spirit of Music,* 1872. Second edition: *Birth of Tragedy, or Greekness and Pessimism,* 1886

Pohlenz, Max. *Freedom in Greek life and thought.* Dordrecht: D. Reidel, 1966

Pöhlmann, Robert von. *Grundriss der griechischen geschichte nebst quellenkunde.* Munich: Beck, 1896

Spiegelberg, Herbert and Bayard Quincy Morgan, eds. *The Socratic Enigma, A Collection of Testimonies Through Twenty-Four Centuries.* Indianapolis: Bobbs-Merrill, 1964

Stone, I.F. *The Trial of Socrates.* New York: Doubleday, 1989

Taylor, Alfred Edward. *Plato: The Man and His Work.* New York: Dial Press, 1936

Valgimigli, Manara. *Poeti e filosofi de Grecia.* Florence: G.C. Sansoni, [1964]

West, Thomas G. *Plato's Apology of Socrates, An Interpretation, with a New Translation.* Ithaca: Cornell University Press, 1979

Wilamowitz-Möllendorff, Ulrich von. *Der greichische und der Platonische staatsgedanke.* Berlin: Weidmann, 1919

Winspear, Alban D. and Tom Silverberg. *Who Was Socrates?* New York: Russell & Russell, 1960

Xenophon. Banquet; *Apologie de Socrate.* Paris: Belles lettres, 1961

_____. *Helleniques.* Paris: Belles lettres, 1960

_____. *Memorabilia.* Ithaca: Cornell University Press, 1994

_____. *The Economist of Xenophon.* New York: B. Franklin, 1971

GLOSSARY

Achilles: son of Peleus, a mortal, and Thetis, a sea nymph. Leading warrior in Homer's Iliad.

Adeimantus: (c. 425 BCE) Athenian general, ally of Alcibiades.

Aeacus: son of Zeus, a god, and Aegina, a nymph. One of three judges of Hades. He was grandfather to Ajax the Greater and Achilles.

agora: marketplace of Athens.

Ajax: Ajax the Greater was leader of the Salaminian Greeks at the Siege of Troy; a huge man, Ajax was at the forefront of every battle, and fought Hector in single combat.

Alcibiades: Brilliant but unruly friend of Socrates. He changed political allegiance several times, even serving Sparta effectively in their campaign against Athens.

Amphipolis: colony of Athens between Macedonia and Thrace, guarding the route between the Hellespont and Greece. Amphipolis surrendered in 424 to Sparta in the Peloponnesian War, and was mostly independent until 357 BCE when Philip of Macedon annexed it.

anarchy: rule by no one

Anaxagoras: (c.500–c.428 BCE) Ionian philosopher, friend of Pericles. Cosmologist.

Antiphon of Cephisus: (c.480–411 BCE) Athenian orator and speechwriter. Mastermind of the oligarchic takeover of the Four Hundred in 411, which lasted three months. Another (or the same) Antiphon concurrent in Athens was a sophist who proclaimed all persons equal.

Anytus: One of Socrates' accusers, a wealthy Athenian of moderate politics who opposed sophists in general, and apparently believed Socrates was like all the rest.

Archelaus: Proponent of natural philosophy, based on air and infinity. None of his writings exist. Some believe that Socrates was a follower.

aristocracy: rule of the best; government by nobility or hereditary land-owners.

Aristophanes: (c.445–c.385) Greek comic playwright, who satirized Socrates in *The Clouds*. At its first performance, it won third prize, but

Aristophanes revised it, adding two scenes hostile to the sophists.

artisans: a rising middle class in Athens. Socrates followed his father as a "stone-cutter"/sculptor, and is credited with a panel of fine Greek statuary in the Acropolis.

Aspasia: Ionian Greek born in Miletus. Companion and political adviser of Pericles. She may have written his speeches, including the famous Funeral Oration.

Callias: Athenian politician, who arranged peace with the Persian Empire c.450 BCE.

Cebes of Thebes: friend of Socrates. Pythagorean philosopher.

Critias: (c.460–403 BCE) Pro-Spartan Athenian politician, historian and poet. In his youth Critias studied with Socrates and Gorgias. He took part in oligarchic overthrow of The Four Hundred in 411 BCE; in exile he was active in a helot uprising in Thessaly. Back in Athens in 404 BCE, the Spartans picked him as one of The Thirty; he was killed in the civil war in 403.

Crito: friend of Socrates.

death: "death is a good." Nothingness or nirvana, and migration of the soul are both ideas from Eastern philosophies.

Delian League: Greek and Ionian city-states which entered into a relationship with Athens, agreeing to pay yearly tribute in exchange for protection from the Persian Empire. After the first decisive defeat of the Persians, the Athenians insisted on continuing the relationship, and it became the basis for what some called the Athenian Empire. Sparta challenged this growing power and the Peloponnesian War was begun.

Delos: Cyclades island, with pan-hellenic festival to Apollo. Every year, Athens sent a sacred embassy to Delos during which time no one could be executed–including Socrates.

Delphic oracle: most important oracle in Greece. The Pythia, priestess to Apollo, answered quetions one day a year, or once a month.

democracy: rule of the people; form of government in which citizens vote on vital issues.

dithyramb: Choral lyric sung to Dionysus by an unmasked chorus dancing in a circle in a theater. The poem's subject was not restricted to Dionysus. Dithyramb contests were held, and music became increasingly important, loosening the poetic strophe antistrophe structure.

The Eleven: ηοι ηενδεκα. Athenian officials in charge of prisons and executions.

Evenus the Parian: Greek sophist.

evil: "not render evil for evil." This doctrine was a pillar of the Stoic philosophy as the Romans received it. Tolstoy's interpretation of the commandments of Jesus similarly emphasizes "resist not evil."

gadfly: large fly that torments cattle and horses.

Gorgias: (c.483–385) Born in Leontini, Sicily. Sophist of rhetoric and expressive declamation.

Hector: Eldest son of Priam and Hecuba of Troy, husband of Andromache. Hector led the Trojans against the Greeks in the *Iliad*.

Herakles: (Roman: Hercules) Son of Zeus and Alcmena, noted for strength and courage. A cult figure for Greeks and Romans. Twelve Herculean labors. Herakles was assigned twelve impossible tasks by Eurystheus, but performed them all, sometimes by intelligence and sometimes by superhuman strength.

Hesiod: (c.700 BCE) Greek epic poet. Born in Boeotia.

Hippias: Tyrant of Athens from 527 to 510 BCE. He abandoned Athens for the court of Darius, the Persian invader, and was with the Persians at their defeat at Marathon in 490 BCE.

Homer: (8th century BCE?) Greek epic poet, author of *Iliad, Odyssey*, and perhaps other epics.

Lycon: listed as one of Socrates' accusers.

Meletus: one of Socrates' accusers. His father Meletus was a tragic poet.

mina: Greek money worth 100 drachmae.

Minos: king of Crete, reputed to be the son of Zeus and Europa.

Musaeus: Greek poet from Thrace, perhaps legendary. Disciple of Orpheus.

Odysseus: king of Ithaca. Greek warrior in the Iliad, hero of the Odyssey.

oligarchy: rule of the few; form of government ruled by a few wealthy families, not necessarily high-born. (See *aristocracy*)

Orpheus: pre-Homeric Greek poet, who became a legendary cult figure. He helped the Argonauts escape the Sirens; his music could make trees and rocks move.

Palamedes: son of Nauplius. Ingenious hero. He exposed Odysseus' ploy to avoid serving in the Trojan investment, and then was framed by Odysseus as a traitor and stoned to death.

penalty: In Athenian law, both suer and sued propose penalties after a guilty verdict is given.

Phthia: Thessaly town of exile for Peleus.

Plato: (428–348 BCE) Greek philosopher and teacher. He considered himself a younger colleague of Socrates, not a student or disciple.

Potidaea: Corinthian colony near Macedonia. Revolted from Delian League in 432 BCE, but Athens retook it in 430.

Prodicus: (c.465–c.399 BCE) Sophist who emphasized ethics based on work.

prytaneum: Stone: "The Prytaneum was a place of honor. It was the city hall, the seat of the city's executive government...[it] had a sacred character." Socrates asks not for a sentence but instead suggests a sacrilege.

Pythian prophetess: channel for the Delphic oracle.

Rhadamanthus: brother of Minos, one of three judges of Hades.

Simmias of Thebes: (c. 400 BCE) Pythagorean philosopher.

Sisyphus: legendary figure; son of Aeolus and Enarete, founded Corinth, by cunning he tricked Zeus and Death, but not for long.

Sophists: traveling teachers of wisdom; among the most famous of sophists were Gorgias of Leontini, who taught effective expression; Protagoras of Abdera, who taught that virtue was worldly success; Hippias of Elis; and Thrasymachus of Chalcedon, who taught that might is right.

Sunium: cape near Piraeus, the port city for Athens.

synomosias: secret clubs or aristocratic cabals, in which members agree to help each other against the democracy.

Thessaly: A northeast rural Greek city-state of plains ringed by mountains.

Thetis: mother of Achilles by Zeus

The Thirty: Oligarchy of tyrants in 404 BCE. They cooperated with Sparta after the defeat of Athens, and put 1,500 Athenians to death before the Thirty were overthrown in 403 BCE.

tragedy: from τραγοιδια, goat song. The only Greek tragedies we have are from Athens, where it may have originated. The basic tragic plot is a high-born person who suffers misfortune, told in hexameter verse. Aristotle believes it developed from the dithyramb.

Triptolemus: chosen by Demeter to teach agriculture to humans. One of three judges of Hades.

tyrant: Greek absolute ruler. Many tyrants were oligarchs who led popular revolts against oppression, and seized power from hereditary monarchs. Often these were resourceful forward-looking individuals, and by breaking with traditional hereditary ways, they enabled democracy to get started.

The Apology of Socrates,

or

Socrates' Defence before the Dicasts

Xenophon

Translation by H. G. Dakyns

Among the reminiscences of Socrates, none, as it seems to me, is more deserving of record than the counsel he took with himself (after being cited to appear before the court), not only with regard to his defence, but also as to the ending of his life. Others have written on this theme, and all without exception have done full justice to the lofty style of the philosopher, which may be taken as a proof that the language used by Socrates was really of that type. But none of these writers has brought out clearly the fact that Socrates had come to regard death as for himself preferable to life; and consequently there is just a suspicion of foolhardiness in the arrogancy of his address.

We have, however, from the lips of one of his intimate acquaintances, Hermogenes, the son of Hipponicus, an account of him which shows the high demeanour in question to have been altogether in keeping with the philosopher's cast of thought. Hermogenes says that, seeing Socrates discoursing on every topic rather than that of his impending trial, he roundly put it to him whether he ought not to be debating the line of his defence, to which Socrates in the first instance answered: "What! do I not seem to you to have spent my whole life in meditating my defence?"

And when Hermogenes asked him, "How?" he added: "By a lifelong persistence in doing nothing wrong, and that I take to be the finest practice for his defence which a man could devise."

Presently reverting to the topic, Hermogenes demanded: "Do you not see, Socrates, how often Athenian juries [dikasteries] are constrained by arguments to put quite innocent people to death, and not less often to acquit the guilty, either through some touch of pity excited by the pleadings, or that the defendant had skill to turn some charming phrase?"

Thus appealed to, Socrates replied: "Nay, solemnly I tell you, twice already I have essayed to consider my defence, and twice the divinity [το δαιμονιον] hinders me"; and to the remark of Hermogenes, "That is strange!" he answered again: "Strange, do you call it, that to God it should seem better for me to die at once? Do you not know that up to this moment I will not concede to any man to have lived a better life than I have; since what can exceed the pleasure, which has been mine, of knowing that my whole life has been spent holily and justly? And indeed this verdict of self-approval I found re-echoed in the opinion which my friends and intimates have formed concerning me. And now if my age is still to be prolonged, I know that I cannot escape paying the penalty of old age, in increasing dimness of sight and dulness of hearing. I shall find myself slower to learn new lessons, and apter to forget the lessons I have learnt. And if to these be added the consciousness of failing powers, the sting of self-reproach, what prospect have I of any further joy in living? It may be, you know," he added, "that God out of his great kindness is intervening in my behalf to suffer me to close my life in the ripeness of age, and by the gentlest of deaths. For if at this time sentence of death be passed upon me, it is plain I shall be allowed to meet an end which, in the opinion of those who have studied the matter, is not only the easiest in itself, but one which will cause the least trouble to one's friends, while engendering the deepest longing for the departed. For of necessity he will only be thought of with regret and longing who leaves nothing behind unseemly or discomfortable to haunt the imagination of those beside him, but, sound of body, and his soul still capable of friendly repose, fades tranquilly away."

"No doubt," he added, "the gods were right in opposing me at that time (touching the inquiry, what I was to say in my defence), when you all thought the great thing was to discover some means of acquittal; since, had I effected that, it is clear I should have prepared for myself, not that surcease from life which is in store for me anon, but to end my days wasted by disease, or by old age, on which a confluent stream of evil things most alien to joyousness converges." [18]

"No," he added, "God knows I shall display no ardent zeal to bring that about. On the contrary, if by proclaiming all the blessings which I owe to god and men; if, by blazoning forth the opinion which I entertain with regard to myself, I end by wearying the court, even so will I choose death rather than supplicate in servile sort for leave to live a little longer merely to gain a life impoverished in place of death."

It was in this determination, Hermogenes states, that, when the prosecution accused him of not recognising the gods recognised by the state, but introducing novel divinities and corrupting the young, Socrates stepped forward and said: "In the first place, sirs, I am at a loss to imagine on what ground Meletus asserts that I do not recognise the gods which are recognised by the state, since, as far as sacrificing goes, the rest of the world who have chanced to be present have been in the habit of seeing me so engaged at common festivals, and on the public altars; and so might Meletus himself, if he had wished. And as to novel divinities, how, pray, am I supposed to introduce them by stating that I have a voice from God which clearly signifies to me what I ought do do? Why, what else do those who make use of the cries of birds or utterances of men draw their conclusions from if not from voices? Who will deny that the thunder has a voice and is a very mighty omen; and the priestess on her tripod at Delphi, does not she also proclaim by voice the messages from the god? The god, at any rate, has foreknowledge, and premonishes those whom he will of what is about to be. That is a thing which all the world believes and asserts even as I do. Only, when they describe these premonitions under the name of birds and utterances, the objects that meet us, and soothsayers, I speak of a divinity, and in using that designation I claim to speak at once more exactly and more reverentially than they do who ascribe the power of the gods to birds. And that I am not lying against the Godhead I have this as a proof: although I have reported to numbers of friends the counsels of heaven, I have never at any time been shown to be a deceiver or deceived."

As they listened to these words the judges murmured their dissent, some as disbelieving what was said, and others out of simple envy that Socrates should actually receive from heaven more than they themselves; whereupon Socrates returned to the charge.

"Come," he said, "lend me your ears while I tell you something more, so that those of you who choose may go to a still greater length in refusing to believe that I am thus highly honoured by the divine powers. Chaerephon once, in the presence of many witnesses, put a question at Delphi concerning me, and Apollo answered that there was no human being more liberal, or more upright, or more temperate than myself."

And when once more on hearing these words the judges gave vent, as was only natural, to a fiercer murmur of dissent, Socrates once again spoke: "Yet, sirs, they were still greater words which the god spake in oracle concerning Lycurgus, the great lawgiver of Lacedaemon, than those concerning me. It is said that as he entered the temple the god addressed him with the words: 'I am considering whether to call thee god or man.' Me he likened not indeed to a god, but in excellence preferred me far beyond other men."

"Still I would not have you accept this even on the faith of the god too rashly; rather I would have you investigate, point by point, what the god has said. I ask you, whom do you know of, less enslaved than myself to the appetites of the body? Can you name another man of more independent spirit than myself, seeing that I accept from no one either gifts or pay? Whom have you any right to believe to be so attempered and adjusted than one so suited with what he has, that the things of others excite no craving in him? Whom would one reasonably deem wise, rather than such a one as myself, who, from the moment I began to understand the meaning of words and the force of argument, have never omitted to inquire into and learn every good thing in my power? And that I laboured not in vain, what more conclusive evidence than the fact that so many of my fellow-citizens who make virtue their pursuit, and many strangers also, choose my society in preference to that of others? And how are we to explain the fact that though all know well enough that I am wholly unable to repay them in money, so many are eager to present me with some gift? And what do you make of this--while no one dreams of dunning me for benefits conferred, hosts of people acknowledge debts of gratitude to myself?

And what of this, that during the siege, while others were pitying themselves, I lived in no greater straits than when the city was at the height of her prosperity? and of this, that while others provide themselves with refinements of Attic confectionery in the market at great cost, mine are the dainties of the soul by a healthy appetite, procured without expense? If in all I have said about myself no one can convict me of lying, is it not obvious that the praise I get from gods and men is justly earned?

And yet in spite of all, Meletus, you will have it that by such habits I corrupt the young. We know, I fancy, what such corrupting influences are; and perhaps you will tell us if you know of any one who, under my influence, has been changed from a religious into an irreligious man; who, from being sober-minded, has become prodigal; from being a moderate drinker has become a wine-bibber and a drunkard; from being a lover of healthy honest toil has become effeminate, or under the thrall of some other wicked pleasure."

"Nay, bless my soul," exclaimed Meletus, "I know those whom you persuaded to obey yourself rather than the fathers who begat them."

"I admit it," Socrates replied, "in the case of education, for they know that I have made the matter a study; and with regard to health a man prefers to obey his doctor rather than his parents; in the public assembly the citizens of Athens, I presume, obey those whose arguments exhibit the soundest wisdom rather than their own relations. And is it not the case that, in your choice of generals, you set your fathers and brothers, and, bless me! your own selves aside, by comparison with those whom you believe to be the wisest authorities on military matters?"

"No doubt, Socrates," replied Meletus, "because it is expedient and customary so to do."

"Well then," rejoined Socrates, "does it not strike even you, Meletus, as wonderful when in all ordinary concerns the best people should obtain, I do not say only an equal share, but an exclusive preference; but in my case, simply because I am selected by certain people as an adept in respect of the greatest treasure men possess–education, I am on that account to be prosecuted by you, sir, on the capital charge?"

Much more than this, it stands to reason, was urged, whether by himself or by the friends who pleaded the case. But my object has not been to mention everything that arose out of the suit. It suffices me to have shown on the one hand that Socrates, beyond everything, attached the greatest importance to the fact that he was never guilty of impiety and injustice to men; and on the other, that escape from death was not a thing, in his opinion, to be clamoured for importunately–on the contrary, he believed that the time was already come for him to die. That such was the conclusion to which he had come was made still more evident later when the case had been decided against him. In the first place, when called upon to suggest a counter-penalty, he would neither do so himself nor suffer his friends to do so for him, but went so far as to say that to propose a counter-penalty was like a confession of guilt. And afterwards, when his companions wished to steal him out of prison, he would not follow their lead, but would seem to have treated the idea as a jest, by asking "whether they happened to know of some place outside Attica where death was forbidden to set foot?"

When the trial drew to an end, according to Hermiogenes, the master said: "Sirs, those who instructed the witnesses that they ought to perjure themselves and bear false witness against me, alike with those who listened to their instruction, must have a heavy load on their minds in the consciousness of their impiety and injustice. But for myself, what reason have I at the present time to hold my head less high than I did before sentence was passed against me, if I have not been convicted of having done any of those things whereof my accusers accused me? It has not been proved against me that I have sacrificed to novel divinities in place of Zeus and Hera and the gods who form their company. I have not taken oath by any other gods, nor named their name.

"And then the young–how could I corrupt them by habituating them to manliness and frugality? since not even my accusers themselves allege against me that I have committed any of those deeds of which death is the penalty, such as robbery of temples, breaking into houses, selling freemen into slavery, or betrayal of the state; so that I must still ask myself in wonderment how it has been proved to you that I have done a deed worthy of death. Nor yet again because I die innocently is that a reason why I should lower my crest, for that is a blot not upon me but upon those who condemned me.

"For me, I find a certain consolation in the case of Palamedes, whose end was not unlike my own; who still even today furnishes a far nobler theme of song than Odysseus who unjustly slew him; and I know that testimony will be borne to me also by time future and time past that I never wronged another at any time or ever made a worse man of him, but ever tried to benefit those who practised discussion with me, teaching them gratuitously every good thing in my power."

Having so said he turned and went in a manner quite in conformity with the words which he had spoken—so bright an air was discernible alike in the glance of his eye, his gesture, and his step.

And when he perceived those who followed by his side in tears, "What is this?" he asked. "Why do you weep just now? Do you not know that for many a long day, ever since I was born, sentence of death was passed upon me by nature? If so be I perish prematurely while the tide of life's blessings flows free and fast, certainly I and my well-wishers should feel pained; but if it be that I am bringing my life to a close on the eve of troubles, for my part I think you ought all of you to take heart of grace and rejoice in my good fortune."

Now there was a certain Apollodorus, who was an enthusiastic lover of the master, but for the rest a simple-minded man. He exclaimed very innocently, "But the hardest thing of all to bear, Socrates, is to see you put to death unjustly."

Whereupon Socrates, it is said, gently stroked the young man's head: "Would you have been better pleased, my dear one, to see me put to death for some just reason rather than unjustly?" and as he spoke he smiled tenderly.

It is also said that, seeing Anytus pass by, Socrates remarked: "How proudly the great man steps; he thinks, no doubt, he has performed some great and noble deed in putting me to death, and all because, seeing him deemed worthy of the highest honours of the state, I told him it ill became him to swagger in a tan-yard. What a scamp the fellow is! he appears not to know that of us two whichever has achieved what is best and noblest for all future time is the real victor in this suit. Well! well!" he added, "Homer has ascribed to some at the point of death a power of forecasting things to be, and I too am minded to utter a prophecy. Once, for a brief space, I associated with the son of Anytus, and he seemed to me not lacking in strength of soul; and what I say is, he will not adhere long to the slavish employment which his father has prepared for him, but, in the absence of any earnest friend and guardian, he is like to be led into some base passion and go to great lengths in depravity."

The prophecy proved true. The young man fell a victim to the pleasures of wine; night and day he never ceased drinking, and at last became a mere good-for-nothing, worthless alike to his city, his friends, and himself. As to Anytus, even though the grave has closed upon him, his evil reputation still survives him, due alike to his son's base bringing-up and his own want of human feeling.

Socrates did, it is true, by his self-laudation draw down upon him the jealousy of the court and caused his judges all the more to record their votes against him. Yet even so I look upon the lot of destiny which he obtained as dear to the gods, chancing as he did upon the easiest amidst the many shapes of death, and escaping as he did the one grievous portion of existence. And what a glorious chance, moreover, he had to display the full strength of his soul, for when once he had decided that death was better for him than life, just as in the old days he had been no stoic to repudiate life's blessings, so he was no coward to face death with no touch of weakness, but with gaiety welcomed death's embrace, and discharged life's debt.

For myself indeed, as I lay to mind the wisdom of the man and his nobility, I can neither forget him nor, remembering him, forbear to praise him. But if any of those who make virtue their pursuit have ever met a more helpful friend than Socrates, I tender such an one my congratulations as a most enviable man.

www.ingramcontent.com/pod-product-compliance
Lightning Source LLC
Chambersburg PA
CBHW021347090426
42742CB00008B/772

9 7 8 0 9 4 2 2 0 8 3 9 9